BEYOND THE HIMALAYAS

A Travelogue of Dolpo and Mustang of Nepal

Prateek Dhakal

BEYOND THE HIMALAYAS
A TRAVELOGUE OF DOLPO AND MUSTANG OF NEPAL

iUniverse books may be ordered through booksellers or by contacting:

iUniverse
1663 Liberty Drive
Bloomington, IN 47403
www.iuniverse.com
1-800-Authors (1-800-288-4677)

Management and pre-service: *Gyanendra Gadal*
gadalg@gmail.com

Translated by:
Mr. Tirtha Prasad Bhattarai
(Nepali to English)

ISBN: 978-1-5320-3481-7 (sc)
ISBN: 978-1-5320-3482-4 (e)

Library of Congress Control Number: 2017916847

Print information available on the last page.

iUniverse rev. date: 11/14/2017

FOREWORD

Prateek Dhakal is a renowned writer, the best bookseller in Nepalese literatures for last seven years. He is the most popular mountain travelogue writer of Nepal where the eight high mountains above 8000 meters out of fourteen in the world are located. His writing being himself a mountain traveler in many different mountains in the country of Mt. Everest, Nepal has been giving an opportunity to feel and have fun of natural beauty for the readers. Beauty of the nature, loveliness of cultural activities, unique mountain heritage, fun with peace and happiness through nature are successfully explained and expressed in his writing lucidly. Readers will be enjoying with his creativity and real expression in his candid writing.

"Beyond the Himalaya" is been one of his bestseller books in Nepalese world for long time. It has been published in two languages Nepali and English. I'm glad to have an opportunity to coordinate on its third edition publishing from IUniverse Publishing. This book will take readers to the real beauty of nature in the country of Himalayas and motivate them to make a tour plan to Nepal which is the Queen of Nature in the whole earth planet, at least once in life. It is my best conviction.

Gyanendra Gadal
Lyricist,
Managing Director, SG Publications
Colorado, USA
gadalg@gmail.com

PUBLISHER'S NOTE: FIRST EDITION

Fertiltrade International is neither a literary institution nor a publication house. It is instead a truly commercial establishment involved in trade of fertilizers and chemicals. In the course of our trekking in Nepal we met such an individual whose writings, thoughts and behavior impressed us to its entirety. Though full of imagination and creation we found the writer was not in condition to bring out his writings to the readers solely due to financial reasons. As we shared with him the brighter aspects of our lives, one of his statements was of an enduring impact on us. Heavyhearted he was saying, "We, poets and writers of the poor countries like Nepal die every day. If we talk about the food, shelter, cloth, medical care, security, education and the expenses for them, we are seriously injured dozens of time and die three or four times in a single day. And we wait our final demise dying every day in this way. Our life is just a waiting for the final exit. There is no charm in it."

This touching statement of Mr. Prateek Dhakal has an enduring reminiscence on us.

By coincidence we had an opportunity to travel together. We realized that this vibrant writer deserves our support. Thus we framed a scheme of support to this person through our company. Keeping in mind the convenience of the writer we then decided to publish this book from Kathmandu and provide the entire amount that comes from the sale of the book to the writer as the 'seed-money' for the publication of his other creations.

Thus the book is at your hand. We are glad to bring out the book and take you to a different horizon of the earth through this book. For us the writer, Mr. Dhakal, in person and the destinations we traveled with him are both significant. We thank the writer for giving us the opportunity of being the publisher of this interesting book and wish him in person and his beautiful Himalayan country a brighter future.

Now, don't you think going to travel beyond the Himalayas!

Eddy Calle
For **Fertiltrade International**
Belgium

Embassy of Belgium
A63
No: 526

Mr. Prateek Dhakal
Central Money Order Office
Babarmahal, Kathmandu

Dear Sir,

On behalf of H.E. the Ambassador of Belgium, l acknowledge receipt of your letter dated 10 April as well as of a copy of your book "Beyond the Himalayas".
l am glad to know that thé publication of this book could be made thanks to thé support of Belgium Fertiltrade International.
l hope the book will be read by many people interested in going for a trekking in the beautiful regions of Nepal.
Wishing you all the best.

With Regards,

Philippe Falisse
Attache

SON- Shantipath,	Tel: 00-91-688.98.51
Chanakyapuri,	Fax: 00-91-688.58.21
NEW DELHI 110 021	Email: ambabel@del2vsnl.net.in
INDIA	

PUBLISHER'S NOTE:
SECOND EDITION

Nepal is an ultimate destination for trekking and mountaineering. Thousands of tourists visit Nepal every year to climb the higher mountains and to travel in the enchanted beauty of the mountains.

Himalayan Guide Nepal, the most successful trekking agency in Nepal, which has provided the trekkers-friendly qualitative services since 1999 for the thousands of tourists who visit Nepal, has now moved to the distinct arena then its usual profession by publishing a genuine literary work entitled *Beyond the Himalayas* written by Mr. Prateek Dhakal, the renowned author of tourism literature.

This vision of promoting the deserving author, in fact, we have learnt from *Mr. Calle Eddy* of the *Fertiltrade International, Belgium*. The company of Belgium had published this work in 2002 first time and also provided an opportunity especially to a shadowed Nepali author to be popular in public. After the publication, this work became so popular that its second publication in original Nepali language created a new record in the history of **Sajha Prakashan**, a government undertaking publication house of Nepal. The English version of this text was sold immediately and the book remained not available in the market during the last four years. We have also acknowledged that a large number of readers have shown their queries especially about the scarcity of this text.

We thought that we ourselves have to bring this work in the market. Consequently, we requested **Mr. Prateek Dhakal**, the author, to implement the proposal. He then accepting our request immediately gave us an opportunity to be the publisher of this glorious work. This is our first effort to publish the work. But we are very much proud of being the successor of a profound deed initiated by the Belgian friends. Our first step is initiated with the publicity of the internationally recognized work.

We are confident that the readers will prefer this work.

Iswari Paudel
Proprietor
Himalayan Guides Nepal

PRELUDE

The place traveled was the same, but Mr. Eric Valley had a movie camera with him and produced the famous movie *'Caravan'*. I did have only imagination and a pen, so I could make only this memoir. I sketched a movie of this region within me and spelled it out throughout the paper. I, however, candidly admit that this would not have been possible if had I not been invited by the established Nepali weeklies like *Drishti* and *Tarun* to write a travel column for them; had there not been *Kantipur* (Nepali national daily), *Madhuparka* (Literary Nepali monthly) and, *Garima* (Literary Nepali monthly) and all my close editor friends to whom I am indebted for their incessant encouragement. And not the least, had I not been fueled by the readership of thousands of Nepalese people, probably this writing would not have come into existence. Similarly, had my friend Mr. Eddy Calle, on behalf of Fertiltrade International, not shouldered the entire responsibility of publishing the English version of the book, this attempt would have gone into vain. I feel exalted to bring this book in this form with the generosity of financial support from **Fertiltrade International** (Belgium) for which I ceaselessly owe to the company.

Dolpo and **Mustang** are the regions where even average Nepalese people have not traveled. Probably they have been explored more by foreign tourists than Nepali people. This travel account is an outcome of the writings on the exploration why these places became darling among the foreign tourists. This will provide a detailed account of the places to all interested about the regions. This is now at your hand in whatever form I have been able to frame it.

I will deem my efforts to have been materialized if the book would be able whatever little information it can provide to the international readership on the geographical and cultural facets of these hidden destinations in the Himalayas.

While writing the words of prelude, I should acknowledge with special mention to Mr. Tirtha Prasad Bhattarai who has given 'this language' for the entire text. I am also obliged to Mr. Bharat Paudyal for his constant support in matters of language etiquette.

In addition, I will always remain obliged to my friends Mr. Shanta Prasad Bhuju, Mr. Chiranjibi Guragain and Mr. Mahendra Guragain for their support in computer setting of the text. My foreign acquaintance Ms. Michiko Hashido, Mr. Akinabu Otsu, Mr. Terayuki Oiwa, Ms. Noriko Bamba, Ms. Mari Inagaki, Mr. Hitoshi Ikeyama and Ms. Shizuka Saito of Japan, Dr. Sheela Jayanta of UK, Ms. I. V. Nimol of Cambodia and Mr. K. Ravibabu, Mr. Ananda Swaroop Verma and Mr. Dinesh Chandra Sony of India, Mr. Gyanendra Gadal of USA, Mr. Radheshyam Lekali and Krishna Prasai of Nepal; all deserve particular thanks for their constant persuasion to write despite they are in considerable geographical distance.

Last but not the least; I would like to offer my obeisant thanks to revered senior literates Dr. Khem Koirala Bandhu, Dr. Tulsi Prasad Bhattarai, Dr. Bimal Koirala, Dr. Taranath Sharma and Dr. Khagendra Prasad Luitel for their persistent inspiration. I also would like to extend very special thanks to my friend Mr. K. K. Karmacharya for the creative cover design he produced for this book, my playmate of childhood Dr. Gopal Krishna Siwakoti for the prologue he wrote for the book, and

Mr. Rajendra Dhakal who spared no stone unturned in matters associated with production of this book.

March 7, 2007

Prateek Dhakal
<u>dhakal.prateek@gmail.com</u>
Manoharbasti, KMC-35,
Kathmandu, Nepal.
Phone: +977 1 4991441 (Residence)

UNION OF ASIAN ALPINE ASSOCIATIONS

Message

This is certainly a milestone!

The milestone of feeling, goodwill and love, expanded across the ocean!

It is the first, tangibly accomplished, literary and human leveled milestone, established between the people of Nepal and Belgium.

This is the milestone of cordial journey with enormous possibility, which can be stretched quite far.

Everywhere there is *nepotism / favourism* and it lies even among the Nepali litterateurs. The friends of Belgium brought in light a genius Nepali author of the *tourism-literature*, who was shadowed by the very sense of *nepotism / favourism* and discrimination in Nepal. This very work of the author has not only been popular now, but its original Nepali version *Himal Pari Puge Pachhi* has become the best selling book since the last three years among the Nepalese readers.

It has made me very glad to know that the second edition of such work, which has been remained as the *Milestone of Nepal-Belgium Literary Relationship* is being carried out by Himalayan Guide Nepal, one of the renowned trekking company of Nepal. It has been excellent and praiseworthy matter of the tourism entrepreneurs of Nepal, which is metaphored as the *Paradise of Trekking and Mountaineering*, paying their attention to the sector of publication of tourism-literature.

In this context, I would like to thank from the core of my heart to the author of this text, Mr. Prateek Dhakal; *Fertiltrade International, Belgium,* the publisher of the first edition, *Himalayan Guide Nepal,* the publisher of this second edition; and all those who are closely associated with this work.

I hope that the reading of this work will bring the readers to a new horizon, will open a new door of experience, and will visualize the mysterious and romantic *Shangri-la* of Nepal with the reality.

12/06/2008

Ang Tshering Sherpa
President
Union of Asian Alpine Associations

UAAA-Secretariat: Nepal Mountaineering Association, P.O.Box:1435, Nagpokhari, Naxal, Kathmandu
Phone: 977-1-4434525 & 4435442. Fax: 977-1-4434578, E-mail: secretariat@uaaa-asia.org / URL: www.uaaa-asia.org

CONTENTS

Contents

PART I

REFERENCE MAP OF DOLPA

JUPHAL HELICOPTER AND DUNAI INCHWORM

I had never boarded a helicopter till now, though, I had flown in a plane several times. And, it was a chance to board a helicopter now.

After waiting for half an hour at the *Ranjha* airfield of *Nepalgunj* with all luggages, the 9N-ADO helicopter of the *Everest Air* landed on the ground shuffling the green grass. *Mr. Ram Kumar Adhikary*, the *Guide* of our trekking team, whispered to me— "*Mr. Dhakal*, that's our chartered helicopter."

We see from the terminal— our luggage being dragged to the aircraft and loaded into the plane, which took approximately forty five minutes.

Why do they take such a long time? It should not have taken so much time for such a little luggage, I thought. I was too eager to be boarded into the helicopter.

After the long wait, the policeman at the gate permitted us saying "You may go." We headed to the helicopter straightly. I was taken aback when I entered inside. What I had thought earlier was that a helicopter must be a small thing, but in reality, it was not that much small. I found the *Russian* helicopter bigger like *Russia* itself.

There is enough space for 18/19 passengers on both the sides and they tied our luggage by a net in the open space at the middle.

Earlier I got uneasy with them as I felt that they made us waiting for a long time, but when I found the luggage so appropriately managed in such a short time, I became kind to them and wished to offer my gratitude.

Anyway, we went inside and took our seats. We tied our belts and waited for the helicopter to take off. The aircraft made a start and took off straightly upward with some turns.

What a pleasure!

The helicopter did not need to run at the runway like other airplanes and there was nothing to worry whether it can fly in such a short runway. Though we are not supposed to fly the plane and we know nothing about it, however I get more concerned with the useless imaginations of insecurity and possible disaster. Whatever I think will make no difference to the helicopter. It had to fly, which it did and soared up in the sky above *Nepalgunj*. As the helicopter flew, the buildings appeared dwarfs, trees seemed small plants and the ground below looked like an image of a beautiful garden painted by a perfect artist.

This kind of helicopter has a problem of its own. If we could sit in a position facing the front of the plane, it would have been easier to take a view of the scenes through the window. But in this helicopter, we had to sit facing each other like in a *Bhaktapur*[1] bound local mini bus in *Kathmandu*, leaving the windows to our back. And, we had no option other than to twist our heads to look outside like a goat suffering from *gid*.[2]

Despite the difficulty in turning our heads, we felt happy as we were visiting the new landscape. I have got the opportunity to board a helicopter for the first time. Instead of visiting our own country in our own expenses, I have got an opportunity to travel on the expenses of a *Japanese* team. I should spend not a single penny even for lodging and meals.

Everywhere and everything is so auspicious that I feel myself

---

[1] .An ancient city 15 KM away from Kathmandu.

[2] .A disease in which a goat turns its head frequently.

in total benefit. Why should I concern with the minor things since my own role is like that of an independent parliamentarian at a moment of forming a coalition government? From that perspective, I don't mind to twist my head, and I'm ready to endure the pain of my neck. When all of those who are bearing the total expenses of the travel are also twisting their heads patiently, who am I to comment on such twisting of heads? If all those *Japanese* heads are twisted towards the window, why should I worry in twisting my own head? Yes, I won't feel sad. Despite the pain on the neck, I would twist my head and enjoy the air travel.

Long live my one piece of twisted head!

Long live my free of cost traveling head!!

In fact, we can only find out the landscape of *Nepal* when we fly in a plane. The cliffs, valleys, forests, rivers and rivulets sprouting from narrow valleys everywhere. Human settlements are seen occasionally; all the rest are cliffs and hills. Perhaps, because I come from the *Terai*[3], we feel that we have a large stretches of *Terai*. But when we board an airplane, the *Terai* disappears so faster that it remains only like a line. Or we can say like a linen strap wore by the old tribal people. Here our flight is towards the north. Therefore, even the sight of the same line is rare. The scenes in our eyes are only the cliffs, valleys, forests and rivers.

Whatever appears, the scenes are the same always. Whenever we turn our heads, there are the same cliffs and hills. River networks like cobwebs and total loneliness without any human settlements. Meanwhile, the airplane is moving forward following a river and now we have entered into the sky over *Dolpo* district.

After forty five minutes of our taking off, we could see a small airfield. It was difficult for people like us who come from the *Terai* even to believe the narrow ground as an airfield; a space, even insufficient to play football for children too, is the airfield. Half part of the field could not be seen because of the elevated

---

[3] .Lowland in the southern part of Nepal

central part. After all whatever ground we saw from the aircraft, it was the very *Juphal* airport; the only airport of *Dolpo* district.

What a beautiful name – '*Juphal*'!

Like some foreign names of modern children given by their urban and educated parents.

For the first time, I got a golden opportunity to touch down on the land of *Dolpo* on 6th of August. I felt a glorious moment of my life as I stepped *Dolpo*. This visit has become so significant that today the number of *zones* I visited has reached 14 although I do not have visited all the 75 districts of *Nepal*. I felt as if I would boast with someone "Do you know I am one of the persons who has visited all the *fourteen zones* of *Nepal*?" even when there is no relevancy of saying so.

And, I was lost for a long time amidst this sensual pride.

We see a small airfield, a small airport terminal and a small air safety post. I am standing on the bosom of the largest district of *Nepal* amid all these small things. We saw rocky land and onlookers standing around. People are very poor here. Everything is poor in all sectors such as health, education, employment, food and shelter in the whole of *Karnali* zone.[4]

The groups of those onlookers come alive with hopes of getting a porter's job when the aircraft lands. The activities of the people increase with the landing of a single aircraft and some clever ones act as small contractors by employing many others as porters. Fifty porters had been invited for our team. All those porters began to unload goods and to make them as portable packs. They also had a debate in their own language to express their dissatisfaction among them. Someone convinced the others and they agreed and after an hour our caravan of porters headed for *Dunai*, the headquarters of *Dolpo* district.

I picked my rucksack out of the heap of luggage, hanged my

---

[4] .A remote Himalayan zone of Nepal which comprises Dolpo, Humla, Mugu, Jumla and Kalikot districts.

tumbler and dangled my camera around my neck. We began to walk as the backpacker trekkers do. *Mr. Pitambar Gurung,* the Head of the crew said, — "The porter can carry your rucksack for you." But I refused. I carried it myself and headed for our destination, *Yukuri ... Yukuri.*[5]

We saw a densely populated village when we came down for a long time from the *Juphal* airport. Concrete and cement plastered houses were there! Strange enough, all houses are made of concrete! I am very much astounded. I had never imagined such concrete houses in such a remote area. But I see the same thing down in the village. This was quite attractive scenery, which drew my attention. Unknowingly, I moved swiftly and soon led the caravan. How was it possible here to build such houses? Together, I completed both the works of thinking and moving ahead swiftly.

We reached the place and found no concrete houses. They were roofed with the mould mud upon the wooden beams. After all my imagination was proved wrong! Still I had to clear something. I asked myself— how does water drain from such muddy and flat surface of the roof? Is it not that a roof should be somewhat sloppy? Or is it so that it never rains here? I did question myself so much that instead answer, I went on asking questions. We found our path just beside these houses.

We reached there. What we see there is filth everywhere and sadly a naked picture of poverty. Those attractive houses a minute before stood as lively pictures of poverty before our eyes. All over the path we observed the children with naked body and torn clothes along with the heaps of fresh stools. We moved forward in utter dislike of the scene. A large band of children would gather to look at us everywhere. *Japanese* visitors began to take snaps of these lively pictures of poverty with their cameras.

---

[5] .Slowly - slowly in Japanese.

Children as seen on the way
By: Prateek Dhakal

In this way, we reached *Dunai* after crossing a wooden bridge via *Dakebara*, *Kalagaunda* and *Rupgad* villages. Arrangements had been made for us to stay at hotel *Blue Sheep*, a tourist standard hotel. 'Tourist standard hotel' in the sense of remarkable cleanliness as compared to such other hotels available here. Though we stayed there we didn't sleep at hotel rooms. We put our tents at the premises of the hotel.

In a trekking team, there used to be separate staffs for hooking tents and their designation was '*Sherpa*', no matter whatever caste they belong to. One of the *Sherpas* was Mr. *Adhikary*[6] who put our tent where Guide *Mr. Ram Kumar Adhikary* and I would sleep. Six separate tents were hooked for six *Japanese*. Very big tents were hooked for all the rest of porters, *Sardar*[7], *Nepalese* and *Japanese* cooks where everyone will be crammed like fishes.

---

[6] .A clan of high caste Brahmin.
[7] .Chief of the trekking crew.

Okhal: an indigenous grinding mill
By: Prateek Dhakal

I came out to stroll in the town after keeping my baggage inside the tent. It is the side of the market with some shops, some hotels and presence of some government offices. This much is the district headquarters. The river named *'Thuli Bheri'* which sidelines the bazaar from the eastern side, and flows with its unruly tides in the river during rainy season. People are washing clothes and utensils. The river is just next to the house.

Isn't the district headquarters threatened by the river?

"Yes, of course, but there is no way out" says owner of the *Blue Sheep* hotel.

Yes, even the locals had seen the threat as I did, but what actually can be done? Who would dare to fight the river? Things are alright as they are. At any time it will flood, sweep away a few houses, a few people will die and it will become breaking news and will be forgotten soon. This will repeat often. After all, there is nothing I can do.

I washed my feet where people were washing utensils. Washed my shocks, washed my face and returned to the hotel after refreshing myself. It is evening already. *Blue Sheep* is very pleased to have many guests. I cooled myself for a while after drinking a *Coca cola*, which costs more than 300 per cent expensive if we compare the price in *Kathmandu*.

Just I was about to go to bed after my dinner at the hotel, *Mr. Terayuki Oiwa* came to my tent smilingly, and in an inviting mood, I said– "*Oiwasan*[8], you are welcome to my tent."

He had a *Japanese* book in his hand. Turning out some pages of the book, he said— "*Mr. Dhakal*, although it's your country and you might have more information about your country as compared to me. But I have come to inform you that there are many inchworms in *Dunai*. Be careful as you sleep. This book mentions the same things in our language." He said in *Japanese* and pointed out with his finger the portion on the book.

I was astonished. They care such small things. How laborious is the writer of the book, who did not leave untouched anything? I was awe struck until I heard him saying— "I'm leaving for my tent."

I bid him good night saying— "Thanks for the information."

Soon our Guide *Ram Kumar* arrived at my tent. I told him about the information I got from *Mr. Oiwa*. "Well, nothing to worry" he said and as we were about to sleep, suddenly we saw an inchworm inside our tent. Both of us killed the insect together. It was sure to spoil our sleep. *Mr. Adhikary* and myself rose turn by turn to see with torchlight whether we can find other inchworms. We looked for the inchworm for a long time. But except for the inchworm that came to prove the *Japanese* writer right, we did not see the second, and slept shutting down all the holes tightly around the tent.

It became a great day of my life. It is today I traveled in a helicopter for the first time in my life. I also touched the land of *Karnali Zone*. And, it is today I made the number of districts I visited fifty seven adding one more. I also killed an inchworm

---

[8] .*Mr. Oiwa*. 'San' is added after a person's surname to show respect in Japanese culture.

with my own hand without the bone of *Dadhichi*[9] and slept in a tent for the first time in front of a hotel. After all these are the records we can create. In this way, today is the great day I am able to keep such a number of records in my life.

***

---

[9] .A sage in *Hindu* mythology who has given his ribs to kill a devil named *Brittasur*.

ON THE LAP OF PHOKSUNDO

I got into deep sleep after I slept killing the inchworm and tightening the tent. I woke up only in the morning from the hullabaloo of people. The porters were making preparations to leave. The cooks had already prepared our breakfast. I also came out of the tent hastily. As I came out, they dismantled our tent, folded and put into a sack. I also washed my face and readied myself to have breakfast.

The breakfast remains quite strange to me as I found a little boiled rice as thin as gruel along with some pickle resembling that of *Lapsi*[10] in a bowl, which reminded me the bowl in which we used to eat noodles. This cooked rice is prepared from *Japanese* rice which was imported by the trekking agency from *Japan* to feed the Japanese tourists. It's just like rice but is like paste that would stick like glue. Therefore it was easier to eat with a pair of chopsticks. Beside the rice and pickle, they spread some green powder from a plastic packet and poured hot water too. I also followed it. In fact, the green powder in a packet was some nutritious sea food and it needed water to be dissolved into the rice.

The *Japanese* people had developed a tradition regarding breakfast. When they rise, they would never move without having breakfast. And how would they have gastric since they have no

---

[10] .Choerospondias Axillaries.

12

empty stomachs? On the contrary, we, the *Nepali* people, would drink around four cups of tea with milk and sugar in the morning and would get angry with our wives when they call for morning meal. We would only drink tea all day with friends. And how the gastric can be deprived from the national ailment of Nepal? In fact, the morning meal did not get the name *'breakfast'* without any logic. It is breakfast, because it breaks the fasting of a whole night in the morning. With the companionship of *Japanese*, I also ate the same grueling rice and our caravan left *Dunai* at 7:30 in the morning. The porters had already left. The kitchen staff and the cooks also with luggage in their *'doko'*[11] went ahead of us. The rule of a trekking was— the kitchen staff would go ahead of others and prepare lunch for the day in some fixed place. They would also go ahead of the main members of the trekking team and prepare for the night stay. The main members were the guest trekkers, guide and liaison officer of the government. In that sense, I am also in the trekking team as a main member.

As we left *Dunai*, we reached at *Daharkhola* after passing through many valleys, and we had meal in an old cowshed. We felt the *Japanese* meal very light. Our team moved ahead after rest for a while. We reached a place called *'Hanke'* at ten minutes to three o'clock with very pleasant conversation on the way. *Hanke* was also known as *'Sangta.'* We were to stay here according to our schedule. But as we had enough time, the porters crowed in a place and began to sing. We could not be indifference, and we too began to assimilate in the team and sang merrily. There was nothing to wait for to sing a popular Nepali folk song – *"Panko Paat ... ..."*

The next day, we began our trek after having the similar type of boiled rice. After a long walk across many valleys, we reached a cave like place formed under an enormous rock at the bank of a river, by mid-day. The kitchen staffs that had surpassed us had prepared lunch and were waiting for us. In full appetite, we ate

---

[11] .Big basket made of bamboo.

a lot. The trend of the place was that everyone had to write their names on the cave rock. Why should we write our names? No one was able to answer my question but everyone wrote their names. I also picked a piece of charcoal and registered my name with proper address "*Budhabare VDC[12] - 4, Jhapa district*" in that cave of *Dolpo*. I boasted with some pride. Is it possible for anyone else from *Jhapa*[13] district to visit such a dark cave of this remote place before me?

"*Ikimasyo …*"[14]

All of us got ready to leave as soon as we heard the voice of *Guide Ram Kumar* and left for '*Renji*' to have shelter this night. As we arrived at *Renji*, another trekking team had already hooked their tents in the open ground. We were confused for a while. What would we do in the jungle? We could see some houses across the river from *Renji*, but it was not possible to go there due to lack of time. Therefore, we hooked our tents in a row in an open space at a jungle beside the path to a little uphill. "Tigers may come here" said *Sardar* of the team *Mr. Pitambar Gurung*. We got afraid to hear this, but the fear fed away as we were extremely tired and felt very sleepy. Soon we were all asleep.

As we got up in the morning, I felt unprecedented smartness. There were two reasons for it. The first was no tiger has come during the night. The genuine evidence was that I was still alive. The second reason was that I would have the opportunity to see the '*Phoksundo*' lake today. I had an eager desire to see the *Phoksundo* and *Rara* lakes. But it remained unfulfilled because of my business in livelihood.

Though not the Lake *Rara*,[15] I would surely see the lake *Phoksundo* today. This very excitement has made me agile or light like kite since morning. And the kite is nowhere around leaving behind the thread. But the excitement was not limited to me. The

---

[12] .Village Development Committee, the elected body at the local level.

[13] .The far eastern district of Nepal.

[14] .'Let's go' in Japanese.

[15] .The biggest lake in Nepal.

Japanese were also excited either. The reasons for their happiness were that of their own kind, the first was that they would see the lake today. The next reason was that today was the last day of their visit to the lower part of *Dolpo*. From tomorrow, the visit to *Upper Dolpo* would begin, in which the correct utilization of their money to be paid on daily basis would begin.

Everyone was excited equally. Therefore, our journey began at 8:00 in the morning. I also moved ahead breathing hurt-burn to digest the swallowed boiled rice. Today, we will enter the *National Park Area*.

We climbed uphill after some entry formality with the *Subedar*[16] of the army camp. We had our lunch at a range post in a place called *'Palam.'* The place was beautiful with a wide lawn around. There is a nice arrangement for drinking water and there are nicely decorated small cottages of the range post. There was also a museum for hides of wild life. After our introduction, a *Ranger* from the *Teraian* community showed us everything with much intimacy. "We are destined to live here, sir. We can only talk to someone only when people like you visit here. Otherwise, we have been living here in an utter neglect" he complained. His grievance was genuine on its own, and was a lively picture of a lowly paid government employee, which shows how his employment has been making him like in exile.

We got separation after long conversations about happiness and woes. There was nothing I could help him. He accompanied us up to the uphill walking a long distance and bid us farewell. I bid him farewell too and consoled him. We moved ahead on the path through naked rocky hill. Our feet moved slowly, but the mind has already reached in the *Phoksundo* Lake to swim.

As we walked for long in the midst of bush, we could see a big waterfall. "This waterfall sprouts from the same lake" said *Kul Bahadur*, upon which I was assured that the target is not that far. But the distance was not reduced. The mind reached to the spot faster, but legs remained quite behind.

---

[16] .A Junior Comm. Officer (Warrant Officer) of Nepalese army.

After all, the mind could not fly far leaving the legs far behind for a long time. Our feet also reached the southern shores of the lake by 4:00 pm, and knew that what we called *Phoksundo* was called here *Shey*[17] *Phoksundo*. The locals also called it *'Rigmo'* for their convenience because of the place where it lies.

We met a *Swiss* woman *Mrs. Marietta* at a small shop on the southern shores of the lake. She was living there as a paying guest at the house of *Mr. Sitar Lama*, for the past two years, and was there for a research for her Doctorate in *Bompo* religion.

I could hardly drink the *'Bhote Chiya'* which is also called *'Su-chya'*[18] locally. I never imagined the tea which was made up a ghee and salt. But *Marietta* was drinking the same tea there. I was surprised to see her that she was totally immersed in the culture of *Dolpo*. *Mr. Sitar Lama* appealed us to drink *su-chya*. I could not deny him and drank a cup of *su-chya* reluctantly.

The distance between the shop and the lake was around 100 meters. All the friends have already reached the shore of the lake. Why should I be late? Therefore, I hurried myself to the lake after bidding goodbye to *Sitar* and *Marietta*.

Southern shore of the lake
By: Pitambar Gurung

---

[17] .Sacred.
[18] .Tea used by hilly tribal people.

The lake is really enormous. Furthermore, how big it would have been seen if mountains of both sides had not blocked it. I also imagined the length of the lake from the fact that we had planned to stay at the upper part of the lake tomorrow evening and was surprised with myself. Placing the bag nearby me, I gazed over the lake to my content and then only I entered into my. But soon I felt discontent and came out with my slippers to play in the water like I did with the *Phewa* Lake in *Pokhara*.

"Lord Buddha resides in this sacred lake. Please do not contaminate the lake." I saw the notices in both languages, *Nepali* and English. I was greatly impressed from the sentiments of the notices placed in the name of *'Rigmo Women Group'*. We saw some women fetching water in their pitchers. So clean is the lake that it was the only source of drinking water. Was it possible to sink my legs here? I felt ashamed hundreds of times and returned to the tent.

South-eastern shore of the lake
By: Prateek Dhakal

Though I got tilted in the tent, the sentiments emanated from the notice of the *'Rigmo Women Group'* moved within me. How a sublime culture has been developed here among people who we know as backward, illiterate and uncultured. Are the residents of the capital city *Kathmandu* deserved to be compared to these people? We, who dump dirt and filth in front of our houses in the capital city do engage in the programs to raise awareness on public health. We organize seminars and workshops, deliver speech and earn dollars. But the residents of *Rigmo* are engaged in the conservation of the important heritage of *Shey Phoksundo*. *Kathmandu* turns parliamentarians into 'rats' who topple their own government. A minister comes in a government vehicle with a national flag and scrolls his signature saying that he has no confidence on his own government. The price of MPs is fixed by the measurement of their neck like the price of the *Tibetan* goats. And they rule all over the country.

What a paradox!!

Northern shore of the lake
By: Prateek Dhakal

But *Rigmo*? It is peaceful and also is crystal clear. There is no grudge in the sacred chest of *Rigmo*. There is no conspiracy and ill-will in the heart of *Rigmo*. There is no sale of integrity at *Rigmo*.

Really, *Lord Buddha* lives at *Rigmo*. Buddhism is effulgent in the hard working women of *Rigmo*. Is there any comparison between *Kathmandu*'s '*Binabi*' [19]and the rich culture of *Rigmo*?

---

[19] .A word uttered while throwing litters on the street from windows.

Sacred *Rigmo*, I have a great reverence to you from my heart. And, oh, sisters of *Rigmo*, I salute you as your single notice has shattered my ego and illusion of being the most civilized and educated one.

***

THE HIMALAYAS ON THE SOUTH

The morning sun-rays of 11th day of August touched our tent. We have stayed now at *Sallaghari*, on the northern shore of the lake *Shey Phoksundo*. This place, which is also called by the locals, as *'Chhaula-fu'* is like a river-bank with wild bushes. As we got up in the morning, we had to go through the usual activities of the day like brushing teeth, washing faces, eating the gruel like rice and moving ahead.

A beautiful wild flower
By: Kazuko Tominaga

We have been proceeding after crossing rivers at dozens of places passing through narrow valleys formed between mountains on the both sides. The path is teemed with thorny bushes. The well grown bush in the rainy season interrupts our way in various places. As we lost the path, *Ram Kumar, Pitambar, Kul Bahadur, Kaji* and *Pasang* look the path laying the map front. The map provides only a sketch but can't show the exact path. Therefore, we ourselves move ahead thrashing the thorns with our sticks.

In some places, the thorny bushes disappear and garden-like patches of short but very beautiful flowers get seen.

Flowers have bloomed in different colors, which look like earrings our mothers used to wear in the past. The journey is difficult, but such are the sceneries on the way that they bring pleasant feelings in our heart. Indeed, the craftsmanship of the nature is really magical.

Now the nature has changed the sceneries, and we have arrived at a place where big trees are around. There is a forest up to very far away from here but the trees are of the same species. They resemble the mulberry trees of the *Terai*. They have shed their barks and looked as if they are welcoming us with their bright white stems. The nature too didn't log behind in fascinating us projecting white thighs as the actresses do in movies. I wondered perhaps these trees have that much intellect which our movie directors do possess. But the pleasure we got from the white thighs of these trees did not exist long. This scene similar to the exposition of the white thighs could remain no longer when the entire trail ahead looked white with snowfall and we fell in difficulty. As an avalanche from the hill covered the entire path, the *Sherpa* and *Sardars* began to assess the danger to move ahead. The avalanche had covered a length of about 250 meters along the path. After the *Sherpas* made enough space to put our feet with the ice-axe at one or two places, our team moved ahead slowly and carefully. We gathered at the other side, when all of us crossed the avalanche. These 250 meters of journey over snow was the first experience of my life. Later such views were seen quite often, and we faced such difficulties repeatedly. Gradually the romance from these things began to fade away. The reason is that when the snow gets collected on top of the hill, its unusual weight makes the part of the hill fall down, and it blocks the path.

This style of *'Nepal-Bandh'*[20] of the *Himalayan* region was different from other strikes of *Nepal* in the sense that it would not harm anybody but rather it would provide a pleasure from the risk of going ahead. We reached at a village called *'Dobha*n' by the evening. At this village called *'Ghyangkopa'* in local language, two rivers coming from two sides would merge here. Today's night stay will be at a garden-like spur of the convergence of the two rivers. The *Sherpas* are hooking my tent at the spur from where convergence is visible.

The sun rose once again. The calendar showed another day 27 instead of 26th of the *Nepalese* month of *Shrawan*[21]. We passed through a long way since yesterday and also reduced own lifespan by twenty four hours from our total age. Death has come closer by one day, but it has been no curtailing in pleasure and excitement of the journey.

"We will across the *Himalayas* from today." The guide informed which made me greatly enthusiastic and I felt it would have been better if we had covered our path very soon. But it was useless for me to hurry alone. *Japanese* cook *Mr. Tikaram* set the cauldron on the oven to cook meal. *Nepali* cook *Pasang* was cleansing the smeared utensils left since the morning with rhythm of a *Nepali* folk song *"Raksi khana jaun dajai, Raksi khana jaun …"*[22]

Our journey began after taking tea, bread and *Japanese* boiled rice as breakfast. Today the trail ahead is very difficult and there is nothing remarkable as there are the same bushes and shrubs; barren hills and valleys, streams and the same tiresome journey with very slow speed! Our caravan is spread over a long

---

[20] .A call for general strike throughout the country.
[21] .12 August 1996
[22] .O brother! Let's go for a drink.

stretch of trail. Everyone is in his own thought. I am astounded with the hard labor of *Mr. Mashahiro Kurasaki* who spreads the tripod of his camera wherever he finds something remarkable scene and *Miss Kazuko Tominaga* prepares a sketch timely while others would spend time in smoking a cigarette. *Mr. Terayuki Oiwa* is somewhat different from these all. He runs after any *Stupa*, *Chorten* or *Gumba* with a measuring tape to measure it. *Miss Reiko*, *Chunoda* and *Michiko* are very carefree. They neither measure *Chorten* nor remain busy in making sketches. Sometimes they take pictures and most of the time they spend chewing chewing-gums.

Mr. Oiwa and Kurasaki with the author (Tokyo 1999)
By: Kazuko Tominaga

Perhaps because of her old-age, *Miss Tominaga* can not walk quickly. She is always at the back of our group and I am still behind her. Only one person behind me is *Mr. Moti Neupane*. *Moti* is a staff of the trekking agency. Therefore, he might have walked behind the caravan under the rules of their own agency. But I am at the rear in honor of the age of *Miss Tominaga* and to cooperate her because of her cordiality.

Kazuko, author and Moti:
By: R.K. Adhikary

After reaching a slope resembling a mustard farm at an altitude of 3900 meters, we looked back at the trail we had passed through. What pleasant scenery! We could see from here the scene of the beautiful lake *Shey Phokshundo* which looked like a small picture, is fantastic. I informed all others about it happily. Everyone looked back and enjoyed the scenery. This small glimpse of the lake delighted our heart and also removed tiredness.

After a day long walk along a difficult path we reached at *Chhorangla base camp*[23] in the evening. We have to turn to the south, if we are to look at the *Himalayas*. Now, we have arrived at a completely closed area beyond the *Himalayas*. It is an open prison. There is no easy outlet anywhere from here.

---

[23] .Called *Myandoktui* in local dialect.

A beautiful natural garden
By: Prateek Dhakal

In the evening, sitting outside the tent, I watched the yellowish scenery of the *Himalayas* of the south. The geography of *Nepal* I have read so far had taught me that the *Himalayas* are on the northern border, but the established truth in my mind, has been proved wrong before my eyes. I practically witnessed it today. I am resting at a *Nepalese* territory beyond the *Himalayas* and my own *Himalayas* are smiling toward the south. What a joy after reaching upward even from the *Himalayas*! Perhaps, to seek this joy the mountaineers climb the *Himalayan* peaks taking risk of their lives!

***

Around Shey Gumba

We had to cross a stream as soon as we left from the *Chhorangla* base camp. Now, the chilling water makes our feet unable to move. To avoid it, I looked around the narrowed space to cross the water by jumping, but didn't find the convenient space. I was forced to take off my shoes to step into the water. My God! I could not move my feet further. I thought as if my feet have been chopped off and I have become a lame. However, we crossed the river but it took very long time to recover the leg.

After crossing the stream, we began to climb a smaller hillock and as soon as we reached at the top, we saw sloppy and wide *Himalayan* plain area.

Infant rivers taking their motion
By: Prateek Dhakal

Because of its slope, I think we can't call it plain. Therefore, it will be better to call it enormous sloppy highland. As we reached there, our porters began to dig on the ground here and there. I was startled for a moment. Why are these tired people running so fast? I didn't get any hint. Later, we knew that we could find here the valuable Himalayan herb 'Yarchagumba',[24] and for which the porters were running to accumulate by surpassing their friends.

I had seen the picture of a 'Yarchagumba' only in a postal stamp, but today I have seen it just before me. This thing is really strange— downwards an insect and upwards a mushroom! Whether we call it vegetation or a creature? Quite strange! The insect with a mushroom as an umbrella on its head and sways nicely. It is an insect shaped exactly like a caterpillar, without fur.

The porters and helpers of our team began to search and eat the yarchagumba. The porters were explaining about its significance as "This makes us healthier, increases sexual power and takes care of overall body. This is the king of all medicines. It has been prohibited to export. One is fined *Rupees* fifty per piece ... etc etc." The *Japanese* trekkers were looking carefully at the wonderful medicine in their hands.

Saying "Sir, you can eat it" a porter gave me 3 *yarchagumbas*. But I did not dare to swallow the muddy insect and put it into my pocket saying "I would eat them later." But the porters ate the unwashed *yarchagumba* approximately ten to twelve piece per person.

The enthusiasm of the *yarchagumba* got over as soon as we crossed the slope. This was found in certain places, and not everywhere. We have already walked two and half hours after we left our camp and now we are at the top of the *'Sela pass'*, the highest point of this area at an altitude of 5388 meters. We can't

---

[24] .Cordycep Sinensis

Miss Reiko Ogasabara holding Yarchagumba
By: Prateek Dhakal

meters. We can't see a single speck of soil from the foot to the highest point of this pass. Everywhere there are stones and stone and its dust is spread as the soil. There is no vegetation at all.

After falling down the snowy landslide, it gets little melted and the segment flows. When all these snowy segments flow from the terraces of the sloppy hills and entangle with each other, they turn into the lucid water and originate rivers. I imagined if our children had been taken here, how happy they would be to see such miraculous scenes. But it was not possible at present.

Now we are standing on the top of the pass. A gentle cold breeze is cooling the heat we attained while climbing the hill. The snow is accompanying the wind. To see snow falling over oneself was the most pleasant scenery. The snow is falling like the fur of *Simal*[25] tree on our heads. We have put on rain-coats and shook the snow time and again. When it snow falls upon oneself it will not wet us, rather it makes the environment warm. But I have been unable to distinguish whether this warmth is because of the combination of heat during ascending in the cold air or the warmth of snow itself while falling.

---

[25] .Bombax Malabaricum/ Ceiba. Generally called 'silk-cotton.'

After having rest of 15-20 minutes at the top, we recovered our energy. At the meantime, it began to rain heavily. Now, we have to descend downhill very carefully. There is nothing on our way except for the broken pieces of rocks. Our steps can't be stable because of the broken stones and round pebbles of similar size. The stones slide down unexpectedly in rain and we control our bodies with a slight inclination.

After descending, we came to a small stream and we followed its bank. On the sandy bank of the river, natural garden of *Padamchal*[26] has been growing as if cultivated by human labor. Really, the *Padamchal* plants of the same stage are growing in here as if somebody has planted at similar distance. I had also seen the picture of a '*Padamchal*' plant on a postage stamp. Today, I could see it directly and I continued my journey sucking the stem of its leaf. It had a sour taste. The porters say it is an invaluable herbal medicine. But nobody knows for what ailment? We swallowed it much thinking that since it is medicinal plants, why not to eat too much?

We had our lunch under umbrellas amidst this natural garden of *Padamchal*. By the evening, we reached at the place near *Shey Gumba* with difficulty amid rain and storm. I had never in my dream imagined that there could be such a grand monastery in such a remote place.

The *Shey Gumba* is rich not only cultural point of view, but also in terms of physical infrastructure. There are small *stupa*s around the monastery and a big lawn nearby. The trekkers do hook their tents here. The *Italian* group has already arrived here before us.

---

[26] .Rheum Emodi

Meadow near the Shey Gumba
By: Kazuko Tominaga

After we reached there, a *French* group also arrived. We, the visitors occupied all the ground and became a good spectacle for the locals around. Just like water turns round watermill in other hilly areas, there are *manes*[27] that are turned round by water here. Holy *manes* stirring round and round, always!!! What a pleasant feeling, when we see such religious atmosphere!

Although outsiders call this monastery '*Shey Monastery*', the local people here call the whole of the mountain[28] north to the monastery as '*Shey*' or sacred region and *Buddhists* would circumambulate the whole area in one full day. They informed us that the monastery which we called '*Shey Monastery*' on the basis of maps but whatever people call it with the popular names, its real name was '*Somdok Gumba*'. Another monastery to the north, located on a cliff, was called '*Charbang Gumba*.' Still another monastery near was called '*Gombochhe Gumba*' and the next was '*Semdung Gumba*'.

Shey Gumba was a popular single word, used to denote all

---

[27] .Small Stupas.
[28] .Crystal Mountain.

these four monasteries. The *Charbang* monastery on the cliff, across the river was regarded as the main monastery as it was a residence of the *Avatari*[29] *Lama*. When I noticed all these things, I wished to visit the place and to meet the *Lama*. However, due to the unpleasant weather and lack of time, my desire could not be materialized.

We were tired due to the daylong walk and thrashing of the rain. Despite this, we went to the *Somdok* monastery for a *Darshan*.[30] As the distance between the monastery and the tent was a mere 100 meters, we moved on several times. But the *Chief Lama* of the monastery had gone somewhere else after closing the monastery. We could meet many of his aides, and we got a lot of information from them. But, we have to wait until tomorrow morning to pay homage[31] inside the monastery.

"Sir, we should have some enjoyment today" proposed *Ram Kumar*.

"Alright, if you think so" I agreed. Then we sent some of our helpers to bring a sheep. After a much hard work, they brought a sheep roaming a number of villages above at a cost of NRs. 2200/– and prepared everything to butcher it. Some of us entered into our tent and started to play *'call break.'*[32]

The next morning we had a *'darshan'* of the monastery. Inside, its heritage was rich. We prayed before the grand statue of *Lord Buddha* for a long while. I lit yak ghee-fed lamp in memory of my late mother. *Mr. Oiwa* began to take measures of the monastery. *Miss Tominaga* began to draw sketches in a corner.

---

[29] .Incarnate.

[30] .Pay homage or have a look with religious faith.

[31] .Darshan.

[32] .A game of playing card.

A huge wall painting inside the Monastery
By: Kazuko Tominaga

Who was the person that carried out such a grand painting and sculpting in a monastery of such a remote place? And when did he do it? Oh, human civilization, your layers are equally perfect when one scratches them. If only we could cleanse the filth lying outside, how significance the inner civilization would be! But what can we do?

Now before our eyes is a grand monastery with dirt and filth, but inside the grand monastery is full of civilization. There is the grand *Buddha*. Peaceful are his eyes and his *mudra*[33] is like that of human welfare. But, the problem is we lack the vision. The ancestors built them for us, but we even lack the awareness and spirit to conserve them.

***

---

[33] .Posture.

CRIMES OF THE NORTH

We resumed the journey to the north, after having *darshan*, prayer and lighting of lamps in the *Shey Gumba*. On each of the hills around, a kind of thorny bush has grown, just like a tea plants in shapes and sizes. We have been coming across yak-sheds in the hilly moors here and there as we are moving forward looking at this enormous but fake tea garden.[34] But the sheds and shed keepers both are so filthy that we can't distinguish which one is filthier. As the *Tibetan* border was very near, the neighbors from the other side do come and make trouble here. The *Tibetans* did trouble *Nepali* people by grazing their yaks and building their own in *Nepalese* territory along with taking away things they could carry from here. As we were proceeding, a man came running away just before us and went downhill. When we reached a little uphill, three men came and asked if we saw someone going downhill. We told the truth and asked what the matter was. They told us that the man was a *Tibetan* who also had built his shed in *Nepali* territory. When the locals opposed it earlier, one of the village's land-lord had allowed him to keep the shed. During this period of 3-4 months, he had butchered and eaten the yaks of the landlord time and again. All this was a secret and was only suspected. But now he had also impregnated the daughter of the same landlord. That is why the three people were

---

[34] .Genuine is something else, we don't know.

33

running after him with an intention to kill the man with some weapons. The *Tibetan* was running away to escape from them.

Though we heard the crime story, but we could not reach any decision. There is no difference between the accent, clothing, their get-up and style between the running away and those chasing him. We can not distinguish who is the *Tibetan* and who are *Nepalese*. After all, here too is the problem of smuggling like that in *Terai*. But while observing the pains of the smugglers here, we can't remain without pitying them. A little earlier we had seen a man climbing uphill with a pine timber on his back. To our amazement, the pitiable man was the infamous timber-smuggler of this area. The locals said– "Now, he has carried only one timber, but if he finds clients in *Tibet*, he takes with him timbers on yaks and ruins our forest here."

We heard the stories of smuggling and that of crimes here.

"What would the three people do to the lone *Tibetan* when they catch him?" It was a natural curiosity. I put the same question to *Sonam*.

"Either they will kill him or he will be beaten severely." He answered easily.

"Oh, do they kill him?" I was amazed.

"Yes, they can kill. Who would see it? Who comes here to protect the law? Therefore he will be killed or beaten and will be thrown away in some valleys."

I was lost within the reply for a long time. How troublesome life and how unimaginable end of their lives?

Sonam further added– "Everything here is done in social consensus. The society punishes to him who does not come to an agreement and involves in unsocial act. Sometimes a man can be killed in mutual dispute. In such situations, the society fixes '*sheer uthauni*'[35]. Everything is measured in terms of some money, meat, wine and *chhang*[36]. Even a murder case can be resolved after drinking *chhang* together."

Mr. Sonam is our *jokpe* driver. He is with us from the *Shey*

---

[35] .Compensation.

[36] .Local beer.

Phoksundo lake. His outlook is somewhat wider because he is literate and because of his professional links that has given him opportunity to know many people and has a good command over *Nepali* language as compared to that of other *Bhotes*. *Sonam* has been assisting us by acting as an interpreter at places. *Sonam* has an assistant– *Mr. Ramesh Siwakoti*.

Ramesh Siwakoti? I was astonished to hear this name and this surname. Almost a *Bhote*[37], this boy's name *Ramesh Siwakoti*! [38] No matter, how I amazed, it was the reality and will not be changed. The boy after coming to this place many years ago with a trekking team as a porter, fell ill seriously. After he became ill, the team had abandoned him and *Sonam* had saved and looked after him and now has kept him as his own assistant. In fact, his home was somewhere in *Arjunndhara* or *Shanischare VDC* in *Jhapa* district of *Nepal*.

A Himalayan old man: the days are gone
By: Prateek Dhakal

---

[37] .One from a Himalayan tribe.
[38] .An *Aryan* name in contrast to *Bhote*s.

"Ramesh, don't you like to go home?" – I asked.

"No sir, I am enjoying here." He answered in a carefree style while *driving*[39] the *jokpes*.

"Don't you like to meet your parents?"

"Since I have lived here, now I belong to this place. Now I love nobody except for brother *Sonam*."

Sonam added– "This boy is in love with a girl. Therefore, he would go nowhere. Well, we'll keep him as a son in law of the *Bhote* community!"

The day is over: we need a night-long rest.
By: Prateek Dhakal

We reached a village called '*Deng*' while we walked chatting. The sun has been turned yellowish. We are to stay here, today. *Sonam* and *Ramesh* began to unload the luggage from the *jokpes*. After having unloaded all the *jokpes*, the head *jokpe* led the entire *jokpes* to graze. The *Sherpa*s were busy hooking the tents. Some of us are still engaged in a guffaw sitting on a boulder.

***

---

[39] .Chasing.

Two Nights in Bhijer

It has been the eleventh day already when we have commenced our visit of the northern part of remote *Dolpo* district and we have arrived today at a village called *'Bhijer'* for a night-halt. We have taken a number of pictures since we left the place called 'Deng' in the morning. We have also talked a lot in various subjects. We have also sung a lot of popular folk songs with kitchen staffs at places where we took snacks. As soon as *Pasang* puts down his luggage on the boulder, he starts to play with *madal*.[40] *Ram Kumar* starts dancing and *Pitambar* always becomes the first person to clap his hands. Although *Moti* has no good voice to sing, he can sing all the songs by heart. While we sing, *Kazuko Tominaga* can complete 3/4 sketches. *Kurasaki* takes tens of pictures with his big camera placing it on the tripod. Sometimes there are places where the scenery is very beautiful but is deprived from taking pictures for lack of flat surface to put the stand. In such situations, he gets angry at the stone and it enjoys us.

There is a kind of enjoyment in trekking. The observation of the views of the *Himalayan* region with rest without troubling our bodies can give us transcendental joy. We have thus arrived at the *'Bhijer'* village with aching feet and joyful heart.

The *'Bhijer'* village is in such a remote area of northern *Dolpo* that it can be reached only through a narrow valley and nobody

---

[40] .Nepali drum.

can guess there is such a big village. It is a big village in the sense that we had not seen any village with 60-70 households during our visit of the *Upper Dolpo*. After having spent so many days in trekking, it made us so alienated that we became to see a big village.

Another attraction of *Bhijer* was that a hill would be completely crossed and we had to go downhill to enter the village. At the end of the hill, there is an old but beautiful *chorten,* from where we can see the whole village clearly, without missing any of the houses, just like in *Dadeldhura* district headquarters from where one can view the 19 *VDCs* of the district.

We looked at the village from the *chorten* for a long time. A canal is dug from the hill across. It looked like a trace of a motor able road from where we saw it. Perhaps, due to the moisture of the canal, the plants below the canal have grown well even amid rocks but the area above the canal is barren.

We looked at the *Bhijer* village scenery to our eye's content. Now, we are leaving towards the same village. It is a short descend and we are controlling our bodies on the gravel.

The trekking agency staffs told us an interesting story about this village. They said the *Government of Nepal* had no information until the later days about having the existence of this village here. Later when a *Japanese* team conducted an aerial survey, they found this village and they transmitted a documentary on this village through *Japanese* television for the first time. According to them, only after that this village came to contact with *Dolpo* district.

Whether this story is true or false, concerned officials of *Nepal Government* may know. But the reality is still such that this place has not been able to experience the central rule. The people call the *Chief District Officer* of *Dolpo,* as the *CDO of Dunai*[41] but not of theirs'. They do not consider themselves as belonging to *Dolpo* but only that of *Bhijer.* The people here have participated

---

[41] .Only of the headquarters.

to build a primary school, which has reminded the rule of central government. There is a *VDC* building too. But both of them were closed. This time a land survey team was residing at the *VDC* building.

After reaching the village, as soon as we hooked our tents, everyone of the village including children and old people hurried to surround us. Everyone asked for something from us. They rushed wherever we turn our cameras to take pictures. Despite all the difficulty, especially of language, they showed their poverty, no food to eat and no clothes to wear through gestures.

A Himalayan grandmother with her grandchildren
By: Prateek Dhakal

The simple folks of *Bhijer* have suffered a lot. They have no option in life other than to die if any disease catches them. And, no option other than to cry if they get hungry. There is a primary school in the village itself, but it is said that only

10/12 children attend the school. They have no awareness for education either. They have no sense what they would do even if they complete their study. This secluded island-like settlement has no links anywhere. Neither the central government nor the district administration is present here.

"Don't you go to cast votes?" I asked.

"Yes, we go in summer, but not in winter" one young and talkative *Bhote* brother answered in his own local accent. We acknowledged from their answers that they have not voted either. They have not seen any polling booth in their village. They don't know any names of the political parties in the country. They know nothing about the political system either. The only *'Bhot'* they know is *'Tibet'* which is popularly known as *'Bhot'* by the *Nepalese* people. They go to *Tibet* to fetch salt in summer but not in winter when the border point is closed because of snow around there. Despite all this, their votes are always casted in each election.

Wonderful! Who would cast their votes? Where and how?

I talked to them about the election of the House of Representatives. But nobody knew anything about it. While we were talking in the day, a man named *Mr. Chhewang* came closer to me with some intimacy. Accepting his invitation, 3-4 of us went to his house to drink wine. He had once visited *Kathmandu*, and also looked a bit civilized one as he was able to use some respective words. While we talked, I asked him— "Who do you fear in this society?"

"We fear the *VDC* secretary" he answered promptly with confidence.

"But why and how?"– I was astonished, because they are the mere junior clerks of the government serving at the grass root level.

He said in his familiar tone— "He knows, he listens, what he writes and in which he makes us signing, we don't know anything, so that we fear of him."

During our conversation, *Chhewang* told us about how things are settled when someone is murdered, how much is paid, and whose order should be obeyed in the village as well as how girls get married.

We left the place thanking him for his familiarity and offered him *NRs. 500*. When we came to our tents our dinner was already prepared. We took our dinner and were about to go to bed when *Mr. Kurasaki* arrived at my tent saying– "Dhakalsan, I need more *Chhang*."

I again went to one *Bhote* brother with *Kurasaki*. He also offered us a sealed bottle of *Chinese* brandy besides the local beer. I hesitated to drink the local beer because of the filthiness and drank the sealed brandy only. But my companions drank both the drinks to their heart's content and got intoxicated.

When we returned, *Ramesh* was sitting alone beside the fire at the tent where our luggages were kept.

"Where is *Sonam*?"— I asked.

"He has gone for entertainment?"— He replied.

We were curious and asked for the details. *Ramesh* said that according to the traditions here, if a man visits to his '*meet*[42], the *meet* would leave his wife for his guest for that night. Therefore as *Sonam* had already his own *meet*, he had gone to sleep with the wife of his *meet* today. *Ramesh* said— "The people of the lower hills would maintain such relations with the *Bhotes* here to fulfill their missions easily. They sleep with their wives whenever they visit here. But when his counterpart would visit them, they would make their wives escaped, so that the visitor *meet* would not sleep with their wives. But brother *Sonam* is very gentle and honest, and will not betray his *meet*. But other communities from *Dunai* enjoy unilaterally."

We felt both interesting and surprising when we heard this tradition from *Ramesh*. We said "So *Sonam* has a real entertainment today. Isn't it *Ramesh*?"

"Yes, sir, that's sure"— *Ramesh* said. Then *Mr. Ram Kumar*

---

[42] .Friendship based on religious/ ritual declaration.

and I entered into our tents and slept in our respective sacks and waited for the *Goddess* of sleep.

I was worried if the drink would give me a headache in the morning. But noting happened to me. In the morning, I woke up gently, felt fresh and smart.

As our team has its program of washing our clothes today, we are to stay here one more day. Therefore in the morning we went to the top of the hill to see the *Samling Gumba* with our *Japanese* friends. According to the local residents, this was a 900 year old *Bompo* monastery.

After returning from the *darshan* of the monastery, we went to the river to take a bath that we utterly needed. The water was not that cold. It could not be cleared whether the water was not really cold or that our bodies needed bath utterly. But rather we knew everything about this island like settlement; along with its sorrow and soul. It gave an uneasy feeling in our hearts- when we thought about the troublesome future for the people of this area.

Author: noting the details before to sleep
By: Kazuko T

Beloved *Bhijer village*! what good can I do for you?

***

UPHILL TOWARDS KARANGLA PASS

After viewing the first sunrise of the *Nepalese* month of *Bhadra* from the *Bhijer* village, we again moved ahead. There is no way to know the dates and days here, if we did not remember it ourselves. The month of *Bhadra*[43] begun today. It must be the time for paddy plantation in the *Terai* region. Greenery might have turned in the rice saplings in the mid hills. But there is nothing except for stones along our path. Nothing green can be seen on the rocks.

"Good bye *Bhijer*, good bye!"

I liked to bid farewell to *Bhijer* once more after reaching the top of the hill. We raised our hands, but *Bhijer* did not reply. The *Bhijer*, which was bustling with our stay for two days, was again lone and isolated.

We had already crossed over gorges, valleys, cliffs and barren hills and at the end of the day we arrived at the *Karangla* base camp for shelter.

Due to snowfall on the hills around, movement of people is possible only through certain entry points during summer. Trade with *Tibet* is conducted from these places. The locals also call these points as '*La*' in their own language which means '*passes*'. We have also arrived here in our effort to cross the *Karangla* (*Karang pass*) and our tents are hooked at the foot of the pass.

---

[43] .August-September.

We started our journey uphill, as soon as our backs were warmed by the strong sunrays of the morning.

The morning sun is too hot and we have to climb steep hill. Is it so, because we reach closer to the sun when we are in the *Himalayas*? What a scorching sun even at the early in the morning?

Because of the overwhelming heat our motion is too slow. With a step, one has to inhale, and after the next step another inhale. Then one engulfs the stick and hangs over it. One deep breath and just one step very hardly. Another deep breath and another step ... very difficultly. This is the real status of our walking. By continue walk, the flesh of the calf has left to ache, otherwise the muscle of the calf used to ache while feeling tired.

Nature itself is like a big canvas.
By: Masahiro Kurasaki

Is it the nose, which first realizes that one is ascending? It exhales a bundle of breath from the nostrils. When the nose loses its status, then it's the turn of the feet to become negligent and they want to descend downwards. You careless feet, can you reach *Yanzir Gumba* when you go down hill? The journey is not always on the easy side.

Convincing ourselves, we arrived to the great height. *Kazuko*

Tominaga, Moti and I are far below but some of our friends have reached at the top. *Miss Michiko,* who boasted in the morning, was lying on a flat stone on the midway.

"What happened?"– I asked.

"*Chukari Masita*" (Tired too much) she said breathing heavily. We also sat there with her for a while. I rubbed *Vicks* on her back, chest and neck, and told "*Yukuri Yukuri Noburimas.*"[44]

We ascended the hill slowly. When we reached the *Karangla* pass at an altitude of 5100 meters, our friends had already taken rest for a while. They looked quite smart. *Pasang* was beating the *madal* whereas *Ram Kumar* was shouting *ku-li-li-li* like in the eastern hills of Nepal, at the highest part of the pass. *Mr. Kurasaki* has a different mood– either he is adjusting his camera on the stand or is lighting a cigarette with another cigarette. He is playing with tripod even now.

We looked to the path; we walked and also to be walked. There is no sign of a plant anywhere. Rivers have taken birth in each of the narrow valleys. Sun shines brightly on the stretches of half-melted snow. Wonderful, places can be seen where rivers are taking birth at every step. We are stepping on a place where not even a single plant can be seen. Everywhere stones only, whenever one steps and wherever one looks. Everywhere around the path, one finds the dust of stone instead of soil.

We have to descend now. Such ascend and descend have scared us so much that we feel feared to see both of them. Our feet refuse to ascend and our thighs deny descending. All the toes of feet come at a place after they are crammed at the front tip of the shoes and feel like prisoners crammed in a small jail. Later when we take off our shoes we can see that the round toes have lost their usual shape and turned flat and pressed. Very sad images indeed! As if the toes do not know they should live in harmony at the moments of crises and everyone encroaches another like the leaders of the *Nepali Congress Party* who would

---

[44] .Please ascend slowly.

strangle each other whenever they get the opportunity. After all it is me, who is hurt in their struggle. There is no way out other than to climb down despite the pain. Soon, we reached *Karang* village in a troublesome journey aided by sticks and sometimes jumping over to control ourselves.

Karang village was a tiny village of twenty to twenty-five households. The farmlands are seen very beautiful like gardens with the crops of buck-wheat and oat. People throng wherever we hook our tents. Many of hungry and naked children have come here too. Yes, in order to mean the bereaved people, we are accustomed to use the term *'hungry and naked.'* But, because of cold, nobody can remain naked here. However, when we see people wearing woolen coat with a number of patches along with other numerous rags; we can say that our usage of hungry and naked has become meaningful.

A Himalayan housewife: life is full of hardships.
By: Prateek Dhakal

Children thronged around us until evening with some expectation. They only returned home expressing happiness in their language when our friends gave them some food. We could not understand their language. But we can surely interpret the universal language of smile.

Today we are going to sleep at a relatively colder place. The cold beside the river may trouble us whole night.

**

WORSHIP OF THE NATION
AT YANZIR GUMBA

After leaving the *Karang* village, at about 4:00 pm we arrived *Nizal* village. This is the place where the famous *Yanzir Gumba* is located. We hooked the tents below the pathway, but we felt unpleasant when we heard about the prohibition to enter inside the *Gumba*. We have already spent thirteen nights on our way traveling all the way from *Dunai* to reach this remote village in *Northern Dolpo*. We have arrived here after a lot of suffering. Furthermore, we have a group of *Buddhist Japanese* trekkers with us. *Japan* has its own importance of being a country providing largest amount of aid to *Nepal*. Despite all this, what would they say if we fail to provide them even entry into the *Gumba*? What would they feel from such incident?

I am just sitting idly inside the tent— but my mind is filled with such questions and counter questions. No, I have to do something now. The elderly people say— "You will win the world, if you have the word." I must go to the *'Avatari Lama'* and request him. My conscience did not allow me to sleep.

I got up and called *Sonam*. "Have you ever met with the *Lamas* here before this?" I asked him.

"No", he said.

"If so, you consult with the villagers here whether or not the

Chief Lama understands or speaks *Nepali* language. Whether he agrees to meet me or not and inform me as soon as possible."

"Okay"— Sonam said and left with some *Sherpa* boys. As I knew that the distance between our tents and the residence of the *Lama* was not that much, I stayed inside the tent waiting for *Sonam* without going out. *Sonam* and his friends came back at 6:00 pm and told me— "Lama says he will meet 3-4 of us, therefore you can go to meet him."

When I heard this *Ram Kumar, Pitambar, Sonam* and I went to meet the *Lama*. The residence of Holy *Urgen Sangye Lama*, the *'Incarnate Lama'* of the *Yanzir Gumba* was beside the *Gumba* itself. *Sonam* had taken me teaching on the way to meet enlightened *Lama*, how to talk and what discipline to follow. I told my other friends not to speak at all and told *Sonam* to interpret well by improving upon even if I made any mistakes.

We were just in front of the main door of the *Lama* when we walked consulting among ourselves. *Sonam* told something in his own language to the man who stood at the door. The man went inside and came back soon to indicate me to go inside.

My friends followed me and we entered inside. A *Lama* with an attractive personality wearing a yellow vest and red gown was sitting at the courtyard inside in the meditative mood. I knelt joining my both hands at the floor lower than the place where the *Lama* was sitting, as taught by *Sonam*. Our friends who followed me also knelt like me behind. For a while, we remained like the statue of *Garuda*[45] at the *Basantapur Durbar*[46] area in *Kathmandu*.

The *Lama* opened his eyes. He looked at us and raised his hand in a posture of giving blessings and made a gesture to us to sit comfortably. We sat on the *Liu*[47] with engrossed legs.

After that our conversations went on. However, we faced

---

[45] .An imaginary bird like an eagle, used as a vehicle by Hindu Lord Vishnu.
[46] .Palace.
[47] .A kind of woolen mattress.

considerable difficulties because of language. Fortunately, the *Avatari Lama* spoke a few words in *Nepali* language, which helped us to understand his intention. Later, when the conversations became free and frank, I inspired Sonam to convince the *Lama*. *Lama* also told why the *Gumba* was closed to them except of the local residents and said— "It's very difficult for you to go inside and have a *darshan*."

Nothing was gained even after such a long conversation. I am trying to get permission for the *Japanese* to go inside and have a *darshan* but the *Lama* is imposing ban even on the *Nepalese* from entering into the *Gumba*. Then I began to talk in administratively as we were unable to gain anything. As we talked, we found that they had some regard for the '*CDO of Dunai*.'[48]

The Avatari Lama Urgen Sangye
By: Terayuki Oiwa

I said while trying to take benefit from their weakness— "You don't have to worry. I am like the *CDO* himself. The ranks of the *CDO of Dunai* and that of mine are equal. I will take the whole responsibility of all the security of the *Gumba*." *Sonam* clarified in their language whenever the *Lama* did not understand. *Lama*

---

[48] .The Chief District Officer (CDO) of Dolpo district.

could not disagree because of my rank. He said— "I heard your logic. Now, come tomorrow morning and meet me."

In the meantime, an aide of the *Lama* came with a wonderful bowl and handed it to me. There is wine in the small bowl and a little butter on four places of its brim. I looked at *Sonam* without knowing what to do. *Sonam* said— "Its *sagun*[49] and you should take it. It's a *sagun* offered by our holy *Lama* with respect."

Soon, all of our friends were also offered this *sagun*. We drank it with permission from the *Lama*. As I disliked ghee[50], I drank it from the side of the bowl where there was no ghee. When we were about to leave the gathering, the *Lama* said— "Please come tomorrow morning once again. We will consult on this matter."

As soon as we came out of the gate of the *Lama's* residence, *Sonam* said happily— "The problem is resolved, now we can have the opportunity for a darshan, sir!"

"But how? Hadn't the *Avatari Lama* given a date for another appointment tomorrow, asking for time to consult?"— I asked him failing to understand the meaning of his statement.

"When you were offered the *sagun* accompanied by *Yak* butter, then the problem was resolved sir! This is the greatest honor of our culture. After knowing that you were equal to the *CDO*, the *Lama* greatly honored you, sir. The so-called consult is nothing. Whatever the *Lama* tells is followed by all. Now the problem is resolved, though I was afraid until the *sagun* was given. There would have been a suspicion if there had been some flour instead of the ghee. But nothing remains for any suspicion. Everything is clear" replied *Sonam*.

When we returned, *Sonam* told us that an imposter devotee who came from elsewhere had stolen goods worth hundreds of thousand of *Rupees* after a long devotion to the previous *Lama*. After being deceived thus the door of the *Gumba* was closed for the last sixteen years except for the residents of *Nizal*. This was the

---

[49] .Something eaten in auspicious occasions /proposes.
[50] .Butter.

reason; no outsiders were permitted so far. We also heard several opinions about the ancientness of the *Gumba* as some said 1000 years and others said 1300 years. However, no foreigner had so far got the entry into it. After hearing this, the *Japanese* team members also told me to acquire permission to become the first foreigners to enter the *Gumba*. They rather agreed to pay some amount for the entry.

The next morning, we again went to the residence of the *Avatari Lama*. He was meditating at his private *Gumba*. This time *Mr. Oiwa* and *Kurasaki* also followed me. Many other *Lamas* had also gathered in the residence. We started a discussion in group and permission for the *Japanese* was given on the condition that they will contribute some amount for maintenance of the *Gumba*. As per our consultations, it was agreed by each of the *Japanese* trekkers to pay *NRs*. 2000/– as the entry fee into the *Gumba* and *Rs*. 500/– extra for taking camera inside. In fact, this agreement was obvious outcome of the secret consultation between me and the *Avatari Lama*. It was better that the agreement was publicly approved.

The problem was resolved, but the *Lamas* also raised the issue of security. I requested them— "Please permit me to enter after my body check. Then you can conduct body check of others as well. It will bring better results and I ensure you that nothing will be stolen."

Thus, after my assurance, they decided to depute 10-12 energetic and young *Lama* boys to guard at the door. They said, "Please, come at 12:00 noon by which time we will clean up the inside of the *Gumba* and make arrangements for worship."

We returned to the tent after the *Lama* community told us so.

We reached at the boundary wall of the *Gumba* at sharp 12:00 noon. The *Lamas* along with a big crowd or almost the whole village were waiting for us there. We twenty five to thirty people mingled with the crowd and a considerably big crowd was there out of the compound.

"Who is the *CDO*?"— An elderly *Lama* wearing a long tipped cap echoed from the crowd. My heart felt a chill inside. What issue are they going to rise again? What a difficulty to convince these simple folks? And there is the barrier of the language to add to the trouble. I began to sweat. And we were not to spoil whatever had been achieved so far. Therefore, I said bowing with extreme politeness as a token of greeting— "Yes, I am the one."

Southern boundary of Yanzir Gumba
By: Prateek Dhakal

"We have something to tell you, come here"— he said almost in a derogatory tone.

Some trouble seemed imminent. I looked around. A crowd of dangerous *Bhotes* hanging long daggers on their waists surrounds us. They have red eyes and are talking something in their own language. Perhaps we have made a mistake and therefore they may beat us today. I was terribly frightened in my inner heart and looked around in search of the only strand of hope or *Sonam*. But he was not seen anywhere. And, how can I fully trust him either? After all, he may also take side of the people here because of his resemblance, in case of any crisis. I was indeed terribly frightened, because of the strange circumstances around here.

Because of the intervention, it was not possible not to go. Therefore, I walked a few steps from where I stood and became close to him. He asked me from where he stood— *"Darshanko kanun chha?"*[51]

"Law for *darshan?"*— I didn't understand and was confused over this question. I felt myself being defeated among the people with red-eyes. They were excited over my being defeated and said harshly— *"Kanun Nabai darshan huncha? Pheri pachi arule dukha didaina?"* [52]

I understood their point. They are seeking something of a written document. Therefore, I told them normalizing the environment— "I know how to make laws. I will make laws for you now. I will make laws so that it will make you easier for a long time, okay!"

Everyone was happy when they heard this. I immediately wrote the fact that we had a *darshan* after paying *Rs.* 2500/– each including the names of the *Japanese* in the form of a receipt. Every one was pleased. I was regarded knowledgeable in the eyes of those red-eyed people surrounding me.

After I prepared the paper, *Sonam* and I only have given entry into the *Gumba* leaving all our team-members there. *Sonam* himself was here; but I didn't see him before me as I felt terribly frightened.

---

[51] .Do you have any law concerning the darshan?
[52] .Is darshan possible without laws? Will there not be any trouble if others come too?

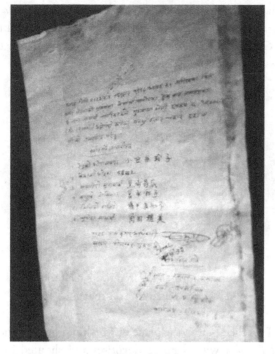

Instant law: a tactful key for getting entrance
By: Kazuko Tominaga

In this way, I got entry into the inner chamber of the *Yanzir Gumba* on 20th of August 1996.

Wonderful, I was totally spellbound. This *Gumba* was unexplainably prosperous. It possesses property worth tens of millions of *Rupees*. Very big volumes in *Tibetan* script of which every letter was embedded with gold were there. Separate '*Samadhi*'[53] of eight *Great Lamas* with wealth equivalent to tens of millions of *Rupees*, nine big and beautiful *chorten* outside, the inner grand chamber of worship, idols of gold and rows of male and female monks reciting the holy books, there was a big

---

[53] .Chorten-like monuments where the dead bodies of the Great Lamas are buried.

drum hanging before the enormous statue of *Lord Buddha* and many other things. No other *Gumbas* can be compared to this! All the *Gumbas* I had described as grand so far were only trifle as compared to this *Yanzir Gumba*.

Nuns: engrossed in religious recitation
By: Kazuko Tominaga

As I reached before the place of worship, I greeted the statue of *Lord Buddha* with a polite devotion and shouted in a high pitched voice— "*Namu Myo Ho Renge Kyo.*"[54] I did not know whether my prayers in high voice would be appropriate here. But I thought that this wouldn't be unjust as it was a prayer for *Lord Buddha* and it would help me to extend goodwill with the *Lamas*. All the *Lamas* only looked at me without any reaction. Perhaps it was a language, which they didn't understand.

I rose after the prayer. One of the *Lamas* took me and told to sit on a seat for recital and they engaged themselves in their own works. It was long time now and I hoped that they would also call my friends but they didn't. Instead, the *Lamas* are reciting in high pitched voices. God knows what they are doing.

I am sitting on the same seat unmoved and thinking that it is late already. Soon, one of the *Lamas* who were reciting religious

---

[54] .Reiyukai chanting of Lord Buddha.

texts came to me and touched my head with something and continued recital. Another one came and sprinkled something and continued recital in his traditional way. In the same manner things, which I knew or didn't know, were touched to me including ghee like substance, articles like musical instruments and some things like ancient books. I didn't talk to anybody. There was nobody whom I could talk to and none who could speak *Nepali*. There was the *Avatari Lama* whom I knew since yesterday, but he was sitting in the meditation on the tallest throne far away from me. After all, what is actually happening here? I had no chance to ask anybody.

Finally, they allowed me to rise only after sitting there for more than half an hour. I walked towards the door. The *Lamas* who sat in rows for recital earlier also got dispersed around. One of the *Lamas* came near to me. We had met each other yesterday at the residence of the *Avatari Lama*, but I knew it only after he mentioned this. Then I asked him about what was being done here earlier. In reply to this question, whatever I heard not only impressed me but also overwhelmed and I could not stop my tears. All my personality was dwarfed before the respect shown by these people. The matter was that I had become the first high ranking government official so far to enter the *Gumba* of a region which was not even visited by the *CDO of Dolpo* district. Therefore, they had conducted a worship of the nation in my name for so long. The worship of the nation was performed wishing that there would be good rain, good crops, no dearth of salt, good grassland for *yaks* to increase their numbers, no one be victims of accidents when they visit north for trade. There will be no epidemics and there will be peace and welfare for all. There, I had become a '*nation*' in their eyes. And, they had wished for the welfare of all including the king and its people through the religious performance treating me as a representative.

A small section of interior part of the Gumba
By: Prateek Dhakal

Myself a nation? I recalled the rule, style, procedure and practices of treating the general people in Kathmandu. My heart was at once saddened. I remembered myself– who is proud of the wealth of his wife's dowry? Me, a traitor who has been the cause of the downfall of the nation by misusing nation's coffer, itself a nation? A living hell of white collar crimes! Myself a nation?

"Oh, residents of *Nizal* and devotees of *Yanzir,* you are the genuine nation. I am only a slave who follows sycophancy for own self with faithless heart. I am not a nation, but I am a termite that turns the nation into a hollow thing. Your worship has been in a wrong place." This was what I wanted to shout out loudly, but for no reason, I could not do so.

Author: receiving the blessings
By: Kazuko Tominaga

Now, everyone entered the *Gumba*. The *Japanese* stared taking snaps. My request for allowing our *Sherpas*, porters and kitchen staffs for the *darshan* was approved by the *Lamas*.

Everyone is happy. Everyone is moving here and there with curiosity to see new things. The *Lamas* took us all around. They gave information on everything. Walking around and looking at various things, we spent almost three hours inside the *Gumba*. Earlier, there was a fear whether we will be allowed to enter the *Gumba* or not. And now after looking everything, there is the fear of being late to return, we had a very little time then. *Saldang*, where we had to leave for was very far away. Therefore, expressing gratitude to all, and bidding good bye, we left hurriedly towards *Saldang*.

Yanzir! I am thankful to you because of your *darshan*. I have become eternally indebted for the respect you have shown to me.

***

FROM SALDANG TO ZANGLA

We had a great trouble to arrive at *Saldang* for a night-halt, as it was late already when we left *Yanzir Gumba*. Because of the extreme tiredness, we slept immediately after dinner. *Saldang* being a suitable place for night-halt for both the caravans of *yaks* going to *Tibet* and those returning from there, a big herd of *yak* has been gathered here. Today only there are 4-5 groups of *yaks* around us.

A small caravan of yak
By: Prateek Dhakal

Our tents have been hooked at the lawn on the river-bank. We can see a small village, the *Saldang*, towards the west. The *yaks* are lying on the entire lawn and in several places we see the tents erected for their tenders.

We have to return from *Saldang* along the path through the river bank. All the hills around us are covered with thorny bushes that exactly look like tea garden. They appear as the tea-gardens of *Ilam*[55] district when seen from a distance.

What was strange here in this region was that the *Buddhists* would offer stones with inscriptions carved in *Tibetan* script at various places. We have observed such scenes continuously for the past few days. In some places, we saw small hills formed of these offered stones. There are beautiful letters on the stones, but we can't read them. We can see the stone-carving artists living in small huts in their ragged clothes somewhere. But, we can't talk to them because of the barrier of language. Like a person who can't speak *Hindi*, faces difficulty in the *Terai* region of *Nepal* and Indian border areas, we have to face difficulty here due to lack of knowledge of the *Tibetan* language and script. Indeed, it is easier in *Terai* because there is considerable movement of people and we can find someone who can help us as an interpreter. But the situation here is too difficult. We find a small village after walking for 1-2 days continuously. We can't find enough commuters. Nobody passes by other than the locals and that too very sparsely. Then who does response the trekkers?

We came down at a village after leaving *Saldang*. Suddenly, we saw *Sonam*'s niece *Tsiring*[56] with a plateful of boiled potatoes. She was with us a few days before, and she left us since the day we had stayed at the *Shey Gumba*.

Now we were happy and surprised at once to find beautiful *Tsiring* before us.

"Where had you been lost and from where did you come here again?"— My happiness got transmuted into question and broken out.

---

[55] .A mid-hill district of eastern Nepal famous for tea estates.

[56] .Pronounced as 'Chhiring.'

"Oh, my darling *Tsiring* has come!"— *Pasang* teased her without hesitation.

The young girl in her twenties blushed adequately. Whatever meaning we did interpret, her blush was entirely innocent. She was so simple that she spoke in a straightforward way. *Ram Kumar* had teased her earlier—"*Tsiring*, you are so young but it seems you have not enjoyed youth. I think you're not 'done' till now."

And she responded innocently— "Oh, no. I have done with three people." We were surprised to hear her. And when *Ram Kumar* asked when and how, she said— "Two years ago, when I was taking *jokpes* to the jungle, three army men caught me and they raped lying me on the earth rolling up my all clothes."

Holy verses carved in stones
By: Prateek Dhakal

This same *Tsiring* was standing before us with boiled potatoes on a plate. The house of *Sonam's* sister was in this village. She had come with us from her maternal uncle's home up to *Shey Gumba* and had come here again to accompany her maternal uncle to his house.

Every one of us picked one potato each form the dish and ate. They had a tradition here to provide food for their relatives' in journey, but, as it was not necessary for us, *Sonam*'s sister had sent potatoes through *Tsiring* as a *sagun* to offer us.

We resume our journey. *Tsiring* was also to accompany her maternal uncle up to *Dho-Tarap*. *Pasang* became the happiest man among us as *Tsiring* accompanied our team. He began to drive *jokpe* with *Tsiring Phuti* leaving rest of us.

We were to stay at '*Chha*' village after leaving *Saldang*. As soon as we hooked our tents, the people here too surrounded us. The onlookers here were defiant, even when we requested them to be away we wanted to sleep. Finally, we could not sleep peacefully until our *Sherpas* got angry and drove them away.

As we were getting ready to leave in the morning, we heard someone yelling loudly. When we watched it, we saw the people two houses pelting stone each other. A crowd of onlookers was already gathered around.

We came to know that they were two wives of a same man and were pelting stones on each other's house and blowing ash cursing in the name of *God*. The husband had left this morning to *Tibet* for trade by loading goods on *yaks*. Therefore both the wives had pelted stones freely at each other grasping the opportunity of the absence of their husband. We knew everything by an old *Bhote*, popularly known as '*member*' around.

The old *Bhote* was the '*meet*' of the elder brother of our *jokpe* driver *Sonam*. He had come here with some *satu*[57], a lump of ghee and a bottle of local wine as an honor as per village traditions after knowing that his '*meet-bhai*'[58] has stayed in his village. *Sonam* drank the wine there immediately as a gift from his *meet-dai*[59] and kept the *satu* and ghee safely. It was their tradition that one had to provide expenses in the form of ration as per one's capacity if any relative passed through his/her village on a journey. Therefore the

---

[57] .Powdered corn.

[58] .Younger brother of owns' *Meet*.

[59] .Elder brother of *Meet*.

meet-dai of *Sonam* had come here. He gave the ration to *Sonam* and explained us about the story of pelting stone.

We again started our journey.

We are walking along the path at the foot of the hill and upward to the hill is a group of women uprooting the thorny shrubs for firewood. The *Bhote* girls were busy on their own business a moment earlier; but when they saw our caravan passing below, downwards, began to tease shouting us from above. Our friends also drew their attention with teasing gestures. They might be quite liberal and frank as they began to tease us from the uphill with the language and gestures saying "Take us with you, we'll sleep together and give birth to your children."

As the girls appeared one step ahead in teasing business, our friends surrendered and began to smile silently.

"Tackle them with you if you can"— *Tsiring* teased *Pasang* seeking the advantage of the moment. Because of the pressure from so many girls, *Pasang* could do nothing and began to walk his own way, with a laugh.

At the end of the long walk, we arrived at high camp at *Zangla* pass and took night halt. The camp spot is very beautiful. This has been the most beautiful spot for the night-halt I have ever halted. Outside, a chilling breeze is blowing. But we have been waiting for the *Goddess* of sleep lying in the warmth of the tent hooked in the middle of *Padamchal* garden.

***

DISMISSAL FROM THE JOB
DUE TO SNOW FALL

It was already 8:00 in the morning while making preparation for departure from the *Zangla* high camp. Now, we have to go through the *'pass'*. A down walk is imminent after crossing over the pass. When I came to know through our guide that the path afterwards is neither uphill nor downhill; it is almost plain, I felt really comfortable. It was because we have already walked for 19 days till today and my body wants neither ascend nor descend. When I knew from the guide that the difficulty for today is only that we have to walk up to the *'pass'* at any cost and then to descend the similar distance, I felt very happy. Then I began to walk ahead happily feeling comfort and rest. We arrived at the *pass* with the altitude of 4800 meters with the expectation and excitement created by the feeling that the path to be come on the other side would be comfortable.

After reaching the top of the *pass*, I viewed the path we had to walk then. The rising layers of the mountains have been visible as if they are in the contest of which one will be the tallest.

A lake has been formed at the foot of the hills with the snow on a hill southwards, and a river has also been originated from here. A hill on the right was respected by the locals as *'Obiula'* religious site and a horse race was held once a year around it. The winner would get a prize of big bread made of ghee and '*satu*'. They said the bread is quite bigger as it is made collectively. Perhaps, it may be as big as the big '*Rot*'[60] offered at the *Bhairavsthan* temple of *Palpa*.[61]

The scenery below is quite beautiful once we reach the top. And what is quite difficult is to reach the top. Therefore we didn't hurry to descend at a time when we are on the top. We strolled around the top watching the sceneries and snapping photographs. We sat and felt comfortable and smoked restfully to our heart's content. We sang in very loud voice and then only we began to descend.

We arrived at a village called '*Tokiu*' by afternoon after crossing over highland moors. At the lower end of this village, a *French* woman had been running an English medium school. Her contribution had greatly benefited the villagers. Furthermore, everyone respected the school as *Bhote Bakhkhu*[62] was used as school uniform.

We looked at the school for a while, and also remembered the mushrooms of the *NGOs*[63] engaged in earning dollars at and around the capital city *Kathmandu* in the name of '**raising awareness**.' We can observe the difference between this school and those mushrooms. The parents of this woman, who live in *France,* assist her and she lights the lamp of education as well as consciousness at this dark village of *Dolpo* by making use of the assistance. What greatness there is in her initiative! Perhaps, no *MP*[64] of this area might have visited here so far, but a *French* woman has arrived here and has made a significant contribution by working and respecting the prevalent social norms and values of this area. We should have been ashamed for it, but we do not

---

[60] .Big bread prepared by rice flour.
[61] .A beautiful mid-hill district of Western Nepal.
[62] .Thick coat worn by the Himalayan tribal people.
[63] .Non Governmental Organizations
[64] .Member of Parliament.

feel. Perhaps after losing the wrapped sheet, one reaches to the shameless phase, in which I think now we are.

In the evening, we arrived at *Dho* village in *Tarap VDC* for a night halt. There was an open lawn on the bank of the river, the west of the path. Our tents were hooked in the very lawn. There was a densely populated village to the east of the path. But all over the region wherever we go, the same pitiful condition of the people which projects the naked picture of poverty is widespread. We began to take rest after putting our luggage in the tent. We have ended the trekking to the *Upper Dolpo* from today. The journey of the *Upper Dolpo* ended at *Dho* village after 15 days it began form *Shey Phoksundo*. And, our trekking from tomorrow will be in the lower *Dolpo*.

While I was playing cards and having rest in the tent, the *Japanese* cook of our team *Mr. Tikaram* informed me that someone has come to see me. I came out with a surprise thinking that is there anyone who knows me personally around here? Who might be the one who wants to see me and why?

When I came out, I saw an old man standing outside the tent and waiting for someone. This is the man who wants to meet me, but I could not know who the man was. He had worn an old overcoat and was looking surprised to see me with his winking his sunken eyes.

"Oh, I am mistaken. I came here to meet him thinking that '*he*' must have come as they said 'sir' had come." –said the old man in his local accent.

"To whom you were looking for?"– I asked him.

He said with an uneasy feeling— "You may not know him. There was a '*sir*' named *Ram Kumar* who loved this old *Bhote*. As everyone said '*sir*' has come, and I thought that he must be *Ram Kumar* sir himself, but it was not true. Now I leave."

I clearly noticed the pessimistic tone in his voice. When I had come out, the '*call break*' inside was hampered and all of my three friends might have been carefully waiting for the end of my conversation outside. Hearing what the old man had said, *Ram Kumar* at once came out and shouted "My dear friend *Tsiring*, I have come to see you."

A strange brightness returned to the eyes of the old man. He hugged *Ram Kumar* with eyes filled with tears. A sentimental scene was there. We stopped our game of cards and went to see his house on his request.

The old man led us including *Ram Kumar*, me and *Kurasaki*. The old man had a house in the village, which was small, low and dark where we had to nod to enter into it. The whole house is full of smoke soot, which gives a strain in the eyes. We sat beside the fire place. The old man offered a *sagun* of wine. After drinking the *sagun*, we said— "Now we have seen your house, we will come to have a chat after our dinner" and bade good bye to that heavyhearted old man. As we came out of the door *Ram Kumar* said— "*Tsiring*, please search for 2/3 hundreds of *yarchagumbas* as all our friends need it, and also arrange wine for the evening. Please take some money, if you need" and handed him a bill of 500 *Rupees*. The old man accepted the money bowing gratefully and we came out of the hut.

After dinner *Ram Kumar*, *Kurasaki* and *I* went to the same old man's house to drink wine. The old man came out at the yard and took us inside after saluting us like a policeman. We began to drink and talk as we sat around the fireplace under thick smoke. Meanwhile, I asked him "You saluted us as perfectly as a policeman does, where did you learn this?"

The old man said very seriously— "Sir, I look like a *Bhote*, but I am indeed a *Magar*[65], *Tsiring Magar*. My mother was a *Bhote* woman and fathers a *Magar* man. We were not the people of this area. But my destiny dragged me here to bear trouble. My wife also died already. Now, I am living alone. I had a permanent job in the *Nepal Police* force, which I lost because of the snowfall."

"You lost your pensionable job because of the snowfall, but

---

[65] .A community living in mid-hills of Nepal.

how?" It became a strange matter to me. What can be the link between snowfall and a job?

"Yes sir, I was a constable in *Nepal Police*, and I came here in a 30 days *home leave* during my posting in *Mustang*. But I could not join my duty at the given station timely because of heavy snowfall on the way. When it melted and the trekking path was clear, it became too late for me. I reached the station only after seven days and I had to lose my job. I could not complete the minimum years for a pension either. I lost my employment in the year 1985."

siring Magar, whom I knew as *'an old man'* till yesterday, drew my attention and sympathy after his pitiful story was listened. But my sympathy would neither help him to get his job back nor would give him the pension. In a country like *Nepal*, where money can make all the impossible things possible, *Tsiring's* job was the only thing that could not be retained.

After having the long conversation with the man whose job was gulped by the snowfall, we left the house by holding the small packs of *yarchagumba* collected by *Tsiring*. He bade us a sentimental farewell with tearful eyes. I could not sleep for a long time even after I entered my tent. Varied waves of thought got emerging in the mind about the old man— on one side there was the old and miserable life, and on the other the troublesome and lonely journey amid this remoteness! How would *Tsiring* spend the rest of his life?

***

REMEMBERING HOME
FROM TARAKOT

We also departed from *Dho* thinking about life stories of *Tshiring Magar* in our minds as he lost his job because of the heavy snowfall.

A kind of excitement has been added in our mind while thinking that now each of our steps is leaving *Upper Dolpo* farther away and it is moving towards the centre of *Lower Dolpo*. We will reach *Dunai* after three night–halts on the way. After *Dunai*, we can reach *Juphal*. Our steps have become lighter because of the imagination that we can fly home after reaching *Juphal*. My heart has already reached home leaving steps aside. There are no high mountains on the way onwards. We have no *passes (La)* to be crossed at all. The legs have felt comfortable, as they will reduce the distance walking along the river bank. The poor toes are happy now, as they don't have to be crammed in the front tip of the shoes and are in rest without pushing each other. In fact, every other thing is normal and encouraging, except for the pity that erupts time and again over the pitiable creature, *Tshiring Magar.*

As we had already bid farewell to *Sonam* and his niece *Miss Tshiring* from the *Dho* village, now, we have only our team members except a few local porters. Altogether the 19 days long journey of the *Upper Dolpo* has come to an end. The luggage of the ration has reduced drastically and the *jokpes* have also got leave from today. The poor *jokpes* which carried our loads for so many days in the difficult paths have separated from us after *Sonam* received the negotiated amount of money. In spite of my will, the innocent eyes of the gentle animals and their obedient nature appear frequently before my eyes. They are the beasts, but without any kind of enviousness and greed. In other words, they are the living incarnations of honesty and obedience; far better than we human. Oh, poor *jokpes,* today we got separated from all of you. The meaning and importance of happiness in union and painfulness in separation with human beings is well known. But what ails me now is the separation from the *jokpes.* I don't know what has happened to me.

Photo: Lamas searching for the rational
By: Prateek Dhakal

We arrived at '*Sim-odar*' by 4:00 pm after leaving *Dho.* Earlier, I was thinking that whatever the name meant, there must be a small village called *Sim-odar.* But when we arrived here, we found that it was not a village but a real '*cave*' between a river and the jungle, according to its name. An enormous cave indeed! Big enough to provide us space in its opening. The cave was full of excreta of the goats. Perhaps, it might be a place for night-halt for the goats carrying loads.

There is a river nearby, nice jungle around and we are to stay here by hooking our tents near the cave. The porters will sleep inside the cave, which is spectacular. I also wanted to sleep inside the cave, but our guide refused and we slept inside the tent.

Though it is no more than a cave but is suited to run a big restaurant. It lies on the way through which pass caravans of trekkers, *jokpes*, *yaks* and goats. No caravan has any alternate spot except to halt here in the night.

"It will be a brisk business if we open a restaurant here, won't it?" I asked *Ram Kumar*.

"Surely, but there will be a question of security as there is no human settlement around. And even if the settlement lies, we outsiders will have some sort of fear all the time. Therefore, let's not try to open a restaurant but move homeward without any delay"— he said jokingly.

The porters collected logs and born the bon-fire in the night. They are now free to burn firewood. Burning firewood was prohibited in the *National Park Area* and other prohibited areas. That was why trekking team used to carry lot of kerosene. If spared, the officials used to sell kerosene here at the rate of *Rs.* 60 per beer bottle, six times higher than in *Kathmandu*. I also saw such transactions in the *upper* areas. The person who can keep more kerosene in his house is regarded richer in this area. Therefore, when a trekking team reaches there, the local people surround them immediately and ask if the team has kerosene to sell.

The next morning we began our journey with the first experience in life about spending night at the mouth of a cave. *Sim-odar* was left far behind and we arrived at a place called '*Laini*' after crossing many narrow valleys and gorges. A policeman of the '*Tinze* Police Post' served us drinking water with respect when we halted there for a while.

Our feet have gained suddenly the speed of a newly married woman heading for her maternal home as we were on way to return our home. We again departed from *Laini* early in the morning carrying our luggage.

The *Shahar-Tara* Police Post at *Namdo* and *Pelakot* villages were on the way as we moved forward. Faraway, villages were also seen from *Pelakot*. Having been unable to see two villages at a time during these days, sitting on the hill we looked on the faraway villages including *Tuppa-Tara, Ria, Bheluwa, Shahar-Tara* and *Gumba-Tara* lying on the hill.

All these villages have been inhabited by *Gurungs* and *Magars*[66] only and we were told by our porters that they are the merchants of *Dunai*. We were glad; at least the *Indian Marwaris*[67] had not arrived here to become merchants as they hold big positions in other commercial areas of *Nepal*.

When many villages were visible at once, our heart began to realize that we were very near to cities. Memories of our homes have been pulling us strongly. Our feet got accelerated. Perhaps it is the reason why the government officials walk 8 *kosh* in a day while going home in leave though only 4 *kosh*[68] a day has been mentioned in the government rule for official purpose.

Now the vegetable gardens covered with green plants got visible. The young girls who are gathered there for weeding plants crowded. The girls working on the slops above the path began to tease us with attractive gestures. We also treated likewise. They also began to blush. We forgot our tiredness because of the memory of our homes and youthful excitement.

We were to hook our tents at '*Tarakot*' today amid many pleasant moments. I began to feel happy even inside my tent with the imagination that we will reach *Dunai* in one day from *Tarakot*, then three hours to *Juphal* from *Dunai* even if we

---

[66] .Mid-hill communities of Nepal having flat nose.

[67] .A caste of Indian people famous for trade and business.

[68] .1 Kosh = 4 KM approximately

walked slowly and reach my home the same day after boarding an airplane. After all, the long journey of *Dolpo* was finished and we were to reach the home the day after tomorrow.

Wow, what a pleasant feeling!

PART II

UPPER MUSTANG

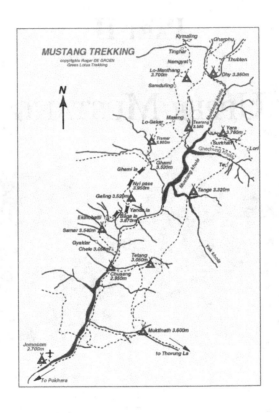

ON A VISIT TO MUSTANG

"Brother, it would be better if I had an opportunity to visit *Mustang* for once." I requested my desire to *Director General* of the Department of Immigration *Mr. Umesh Prasad Mainali*, when the telephone was answered.

"Why do you go? Is there anything special?" he asked.

"Nothing special brother, but it will give me expenses for the *Dashain*[69] festival and it will also make the districts I have so far visited to 61. This is why I remembered you when you are there."

"Okay, please bring your departmental approval, I will send you as soon as possible."

Then I was engaged in acquiring the departmental approval. The process began with the submission of my application to the *Director General* of the *Department of Postal Services*, its recommendation to the *Ministry of Information and Communications* and opinions of the concerning *Section Officer, Under Secretary* and *Joint Secretary* on the recommendation moving with a very slow motion and reached finally to the *Secretary* of the *Ministry*. After the approval mark '*sadar*'[70] by *Mr. Shreeram Poudel*, the *Secretary* of the Ministry, a letter was prepared to the *Department of Immigration* stating that there will be '*no objection if deputed.*' I hurried with the letter and handed

---

[69] .The greatest festival of the Hindus.

[70] .Approved.

it to the *Deputy Director* of the Department of Immigration *Mr. Bhola Siwakoti*, on the very day. Now I was freed from my Department and waited counting days for the decision of the *Department of Immigration* to send me to *Mustang*.

A week later, one evening I received a phone call at my residence from *Mr. Bhola Siwakoti* in which he said that I was appointed *Liaison Officer* of a team of four *Belgian* nationals going on a visit to *Mustang* through the *Green Lotus Trekking Pvt. Ltd.* There were some days for our departure; but *Mr. Siwakoti* had informed me after finalizing the processes because of affection. His phone call made me delighted and from that evening, at my home, I began discuss about *Mustang* with my family members. The next day we bought cold cream, chip stick, scarf, bag, trekking shoes and other necessary goods for me. Beside these stuffs, shaving set, tooth brush, paste, vest, underwear, socks, pen and note book, things like *Chinese* balm, *Sancho*[71] and some other medicines were also packed in my bag and I waited for the day of departure.

Finally, the day also came. *Mr. Sewak Pokharel* of the trekking company telephoned me to be ready to leave at hotel *Marshyangdi* at *Thamel* at sharp 7.00 in the morning on Tuesday, 19th of September. Thinking that it was not good to be late while dealing with foreigners, I caught a taxi from *Babarmahal* and entered the hotel lobby five minutes before 7:00. But, surprisingly, I found none there; neither the foreigners nor the trekking organizers. I am the only one drifting here and there in the lobby.

After a long wait, *Mr. Mingma Lama* of the trekking agency arrived at the hotel at quarter to eight. He was introduced to me first time along with the foreigners. After all, we had tea together and left for *Pokhara* in a small tourist-standard vehicle.

As we reached a little downwards after passing through *Thankot*, we saw the terrible scene of an accident, which moved

---

[71] .Sancho is a common Nepalese medicine for many difficulties, such as common cold, Body ache and other uneasiness.

my heart. A truck had over-turned and was lying on a paddy field below the road. We could clearly see the traces made on the slope by the falling truck. An injured person was brought to the road and was lying on the ground. Perhaps he is the driver and people are trying to stop vehicles to send him to *Kathmandu* for treatment. But none of the vehicles have a comfortable space.

I looked at him. He was a half-dead man. Strewn with soil and wounded in tens of places. The poor fellow may die if he had not got immediate treatment. But there is nothing we can do. Soon the *Police* told us to remove our vehicle immediately. Then we were not allowed to stay there, and we boarded on the van expressing silence, which reflected unexplainable best wishes and love to the injured.

Now a day, plenty of restaurants of tourist standard have opened along the highway. As we were nearing *Damauli*[72], we entered into the *Green Park Highway Restaurant* located in between the paddy field and had our lunch. It was a coincidence that we had our lunch at *Green Park* while on a work for the *Green Lotus*, but that too amid greenery of rice plants just bloomed.

We reached *Pokhara*, but we had nothing to do after reaching there. I was totally free after keeping my bag in Room No.116 of the *Base Camp Resort* at *Lakeside*. The flight to *Jomsom* will be for tomorrow. I was totally free. What should I do then? Therefore, I caught a taxi and went to the *Pokhara Sub-metropolis Office*, my former office, like a newly married *Nepali* women going to their maternal home. My visit made all of the staffs of the Sub-metropolis office extremely happy as they found me there, suddenly. Perhaps, I had done something good during my term. All of them showed much affection. After having a cold drink at the *UBS*[73] section on *Mr. Omraj Poudel's* request, *Sub-inspector* of City Police *Mr. Basanta Chalise* offered a '*paan*'[74] and he left me

---

[72] .Headquarters of Tanahun district.

[73] .Urban Basic Services.

[74] .A betel leaf with spices.

in the resort. I was still free, and had nothing to do at the time. Therefore, I strolled until 7:00 pm and had my dinner. Then I lay on the bed of the resort costed 75 US dollars per night, with a plan to rise early in the morning tomorrow.

As per our program, we had to fly *Jomsom* from *Pokhara* on the 20th of September 2000. Actually we were given 05:00 as the airport time, but we reached the airport in a taxi very early in the morning. The gate of the airport would only be opened at 5.30 am. We just got to enter into the airport after spending half an hour on the culvert of the road. We entered the airport hall after getting our boarding passes following our checking of tickets and weighing of luggage.

But our mere entry into the departure hall may not bring expected result. The airline people say *Jomsom* has a bad weather; therefore, not a single plane has flown until now. There are five twin otter aircrafts parked in a row at the airport, and all of them were waiting for the weather to be improved. Perhaps there is no improvement in the weather as not a single plane has taken off.

Contrary to our expectations, we had to hear information of cancellation of the flights one by one. The passengers began to return. But our *Shangrila Air* neither flies the plane nor cancels the flight. We are confused and remained alert facing each other.

"The plane might not take off" *Tashi* came to us and said. We also saw through the window screen our luggage being brought back without any announcement. We came out, but the man at the concerned airline counter said— "Please stay inside; we will make a last attempt."

Again we saw the trolley of our luggage being dragged inside. A little of hope was aroused in us to see our luggage being dragged inside. They told us to stay inside and said, "We will make a last try." But there was a little fear amid this hope as none of the planes have taken off; it is only our plane was trying to fly. Aren't we being invited by our deaths?

The plane was determined to fly— the plane of *Shangrila*

Air only. We were told to sit in the plane. We hastily boarded the plane carrying our hand bags. The plane took off at sharp 9:00 am and soared up above the cloud.

The duration of the *Pokhara– Jomsom* flight is only 20 minutes, but the plane has not landed even after 23 minutes. There is a black cloud all around and nothing can be seen. Finally, without any hope for landing, the plane returned to *Pokhara* after making a round over the sky of *Jomsom*. However, we were contented that though we could not land at *Jomsom*, we could arrive to *Pokhara* without any harm. But this happiness did not last longer. It rather put me in a difficulty. When it was certain that we flew, *Tashi* and *Maili* had already returned and I couldn't meet *Mr. Furba Sherpa*[75] who was waiting for us at *Jomsom*. Now, the difficult type of responsibility of all these foreigners had fallen on me.

What should I do now? We returned to the same *Base Camp Resort* in two taxies after re-setting our tickets for tomorrow's flight. We stayed in the same rooms as yesterday. Indeed, there was no need for me to pay Rs. 300/– for *'Dal–Bhat*[76] while staying in a 75 dollar room. I could go to the *Sub-metropolis* office of *Pokhara*, or its guest house, or to the *Regional Postal Directorate* or could stay at *Miss Nar Kumari Gurung*'s house as a guest. I had many other friends too, where I could stay. I could go to sister *Mrs. Ganga Baral*'s, *Mr. Ravi Kafle*'s or *Mr. Narahari Baral*'s house. But my foreign friends would not let me go. As they straight forwardly told me, "Please do not leave us here alone," this closed all the doors of the happy reunion with old friends and enjoy free lodgings for me. I was compelled to stay at the *Base Camp Resort* reluctantly.

With a downcast face, I went to the office of the *Regional Postal Directorate* to meet *Mr. Govinda Panthi*. I again went to the *Sub-metropolis* office and took photographs of women staffs.

---

[75] .Sardar of the trekking team.

[76] .Popular Nepali food.

A kind of affection was aroused in me towards this uniform as it was introduced during my tenure. I again met all the staffs and chatted with them. Once again Engineer *Mr. Chandra Kafle* reached me at the resort to the '*base camp*' waiting for a good weather.

I turned on the television lazily. There were live transmissions of the *Sydney Olympics* with the competition of weight lifting and swimming. But there would be no desire to watch such events when the mind was not comfortable. Even the announcements of Medals won by various countries would cause an abrupt anger. *Nepal* is always first from the bottom of the list. We hear that two dozen officials with their wives have gone to visit *Sydney* with only five sportsmen in their team. It would have been better if they gave the amount to the sportsperson as their salaries, which would at least have been an encouragement to them. I didn't want to watch the TV. Why should I watch the defamation of one's own country by giving a pain on the eyes? Forget the talk of going to *Australia*, but I could not even reach *Jomsom*. All my efforts got failed to take me to heights. My plight is– yesterday in the *Base Camp* and today in the '*base camp*' too.

***

LASHED BY STRONG
WINDS AT KAGBENI

Suddenly, *Patrick* knocked my door when I was about to sleep after dinner. He was worried as how to reach to the airport tomorrow morning (22 Sep. 2000) with the heavy luggage as the nine leftist parties have called *Nepal-bandh*. We had to reach the airport at 7:00 am from *Lakeside* to catch our flight to *Jomsom*. And there was no possibility of any vehicles to be run. Worrying with the *Nepal-bandh*, *Patrick* had asked a taxi driver in the day, "Do you have any idea about reaching the airport tomorrow morning?"

The driver had said, "Please inform my elder brother at 9.30 pm on the phone. If you call me, I can take you from the hotel at 04:00 for which the charge will be *NRs*.1500/–."

Patrick revealed me everything and he insisted to contact the driver's brother. I told him that it was so dangerous to drive a taxi at night as tomorrow's '*Bandh*[77] was called by nine left parties and was supported by the underground *CPN*[78] (*Maoist*). In addition, the distance from the hotel to the airport is 20 minute even if we walk slowly. It would not be good to spend *NRs*. 1500. And he was convinced when I said that what we would do on the empty

---

[77] .Strike.
[78] .Communist Party of Nepal.

street since 4:00 am to fly at 8:00 am. But the problem was still intact. "I agree to you that what you said is alright but how to reach the airport?" He was still curious to know.

"Please don't worry about this. I will resolve it after we meet at the lobby tomorrow at 06:00" I said. He agreed reluctantly and went to sleep. But really, how to reach the airport tomorrow morning? It was not a matter of walking of 20/25 minute but that was due to the very heavy bags, which the foreigners had with them.

All the four of them had already arrived at the lobby when I reached there at 06:00 in the morning. I went to the road to see whether any vehicles were plying. There was no sign of a vehicle plying. Not even an ant was running on the street.

Soon I returned to the counter and requested *Mr. Hari Bhandari* who was on duty there to send two room-boys to the airport. He agreed. The two boys proceeded with those heavy bags. We indeed reached the airport in 20 minutes, even if we walked slowly. All our problems were solved. *Patrick* also smiled now after a long time. We were at the airport before airport time in spite of the morning walk on the very day of strong *Nepal-bandh* day.

The planes were flying. In its third flight to *Jomsom* the *Shangrila Air* lifted us and flew with signs that it will really land at *Jomsom* today. The sky is clear and the view around is also very clear. From the windows of the plane, we can see the houses below no bigger than the small dots, and also the green forests, empty grassland inside the jungles, cliffs, valleys, and sparsely populated villages and the *Kaligandaki River*'s *gorge* [79] that has left only enough breadth to fly a plane. Our plane is flying between the cliffs with the space hardly enough on either sides. The plane had just come out of the gorge and we had already reached *Jomsom*. When I was only looking for the airport from the window with a stretch of my head, the wheel of the aero plane had already blown away dust on the airfield.

---

[79] .The deepest gorge in the world.

We got out with a new vigor and enthusiasm. *Sardar Mr. Furba Wangdi Sherpa* and others were waiting for us to welcome. They carried our bags and took us to the *'Moonlight restaurant'*.

As soon as we put our bags at the *Moonlight*, I came out to take a view of *Jomsom*. Everything including lodges and restaurants had a new look and standard because of the tourism industry. Caravans of mules and the piles of firewood on roofs were new to me. I went a little far away, returned back and looked at *Jomsom* to my eyes' content. The tractors carried by aircrafts to build the airport are carrying construction material from the river banks. Caravans of mules with big bells hanging are either coming or going. It is about to 10:00 and the gust of wind is supposed to begin. Anyway, the music of life is sounded in *Jomsom* because of this airport.

Breakfast was ready. We began to eat at a big table whose underneath was also curtained.

We were told that our destination today was not that far, therefore we began our journey along the banks of *Kaligandaki River* after a long rest.

We are walking on the banks of *Kaligandaki*. The wind has begun to blow so forcefully that it is pushing us on our backs. If we take one step forward the wind would push the other.

After walking three hours through the western banks of *Kaligandaki,* we reached at the place of suspension bridge, and crossing through the bridge, we arrived at the eastern bank. While crossing the river; we were lashed at hundreds of times by the wind. But it was not rational to accuse him in his own place. Therefore, we silently crossed the bridge and entered into a restaurant at *Eklebhati* to have lunch. The restaurant is clean and very tidily decorated, but none of the doors or windows is open. Now it was clear to me, the windows and doors were closed to protect rooms from dust because of the wind. In these lodges and restaurants which are opened to serve the tourists as well as their owners, have windows with big glasses which provide enough light in the rooms without opening them. The open windows will let the big specks of sands to be entered inside the rooms from the riverbanks.

There are fourteen men and eight mules in our group. We are slowly proceeding towards *'Kagbeni'*. The path ahead is not that long for us to reach to the place of our night stay. *'Kagbeni'* is just visible to our eyes. But now the wind is blowing so strongly that it will blow us off the road if we do not walk carefully. There is no way other than to clutch the cap with one of our hands. Only one hand is free to sway forward when one hand is engaged in holding our caps. It has made us uncomfortable as we have lost our balance due to the lack of swaying both the hands. You might say– it's not a problem for us who do not wear caps. But the reality is different. We can have headaches because of the continual thrust of wind on one side and the scorching heat on the other. Therefore, it is obligatory to everyone who comes from the *south* to wear a cap. And isn't one of your hands engaged vainly in holding your cap?

As soon as we proceed ahead from *Jomsom*, Mount *Tilicho* (7134 m) and Mount *Nilgiri* (6940 m) *Himalayas* are visible to the south from the *Kaligandaki* river-banks. Though invisible from the path, the ridges of Mount *Dhaulagiri* and Mount *Annapurna Himalayas* remain back to the south. This journey happens to be purely of the region beyond the *Himalayas*, which begins as soon as we land at the *Jomsom* airport. But the journey from *Eklebhati* to *Kagbeni* is more enchanting with the *Himalayan* scenery and the Himalayan peaks on both north and south sides. How pleasant it is to walk between full of *Himalayan* peaks!

As we reached a little above *Eklebhati*, we saw a beautiful spot resembling a garden with some trees. These trees naturally drew our attention, as we didn't see any trees for a long time. The ramified trees! They were *'saur'*[80] trees planted and grown up later.

After we arrived at *Kagbeni*, we decided to stay tonight. Although it's only 14:00, we decided not to proceed ahead. We kept our luggage in a room of *'Everest Guest House'* and went to

---

[80] .Birch trees, Betula Alnoides.

see the "*Kag Chode Thupten Samphel Ling*" monastery at *Kagbeni* with my *Belgian* friends.

The monastery is simple. From its roof-top some dilapidated houses were seen nearby as if collapsed in earthquake. When we went to see it, we found there was a path under those ruined houses. Deep inside the path would divide into many small alleys and each alley ended at a door step of each house. When we entered inside further, we saw nice path paved with stone-slaps and what we saw there were nice lodges and restaurants with signboards. Finally, the small path under the rubble merged with the main road and led us to the same lodge where we were to stay that night. We were pleased with the joyful feeling. Had we not gone to see the monastery, we would have been deprived of seeing the rubble like man made underground tunnel and the settlement tangled with it.

Kag Chode Thupten Samphel Ling Gumba in Kagbeni
Byo: Prateek Dhakal

Another group had already put up tents where there was a wall to support it. We had no space for it. Therefore we decided to sleep in the rooms of the lodge. In *Mustang*, there is no possibility of putting up tents in open space wherever we like as in trekking elsewhere because of the strong wind. Moreover, *Kagbeni* has a wind mill owned by the *Nepal Electricity Authority*. Therefore the lodge owners surround spaces by walls to put up tents. We got no space and it brought everything to an end. Our friends had made arrangements for foreigners to sleep in first floor rooms and for we *Gurkhas*,[81] in the ground floor.

Our cook *Mr. Roop Lama* served us evening meal which consisted of garlic chicken soup, boiled vegetable, pizza, momo, finger chips and boiled fruits. The skills of our cook were no less than any standard star hotels. For the first night today, we had our meal called 'dinner' prepared by him. For many days we will have breakfast, lunch and dinner prepared by him. But howsoever skillfully he has made or whatsoever hygienically it is made, it could not be so delicious, full of salt and sour, fat and chilly, quite tasteful to the tongue of *Gurkhas*.

Photo: Kids: trekkers of the future.
By: Prateek Dhakal

***

---

[81] Nepali people are also called 'Gurkhas' because of their bravery and origination.

IN SEARCH OF SHALIGRAM

We had the opportunity to see the golden face of the *Mount Nilgiri* from the very gate of the hotel as soon as we got up from the bed. On the one hand, I have got the opportunity to see it to the south whereas we are on the north, that too from the very door of the house and that too a golden mountain having the touch of the young sun. How can we explain in words about such perfect beauty and transcendental bliss emerged in us?

For the first time in my life today, on 22nd of September 2000, the words of a lyrics written by *Mr. Kali Prasad Rijal* have come to be relevant. *"Bihana Uthne Bittikai Himal Dekhna Paaiyos."*[82]

How was this feeling arisen in the poet *Kali Prasadji?*[83] Did he write these lines of this song with the pre-assumption of the feeling of glory that has enchanted me with the mere watching of the *Himalayas?* Did he write the song for the expression of the same feeling that has arisen in me as I see the *Himalaya* now just after I rise?

Things kept on emerging in my mind and my sentiments were inter-mingled with the feeling of the lyricist. But more necessary was to show this rare and golden scene to the foreign friends. Therefore, I hastily went inside and showed them all one

---

[82] .Let the Himalayas be seen just after rising from the bed.
[83] .'Ji' is added after a person's name to show respect in Nepali culture.

by one. *Mr. Calle Eddy* was the only one who missed to see it. When *Eddy* came down, the *Himalaya* had already turned silvery. *Eddy* who had heard of golden peaks only got the chance to see the silver peaks.

We had our breakfast while talking about the *Himalayas*. How pleasant it was to have breakfast while talking about the *Himalayan* peaks. Only today I got the opportunity to experience this. While talking about trekking, taking breakfast means starting journey for the day. We began our journey again. We were registered at the *check-post* of the *ACAP*[84] after we entered through a cave like an alley. We left our video camera after receiving a receipt and moved ahead with an ordinary photographic camera.

Panoramic view of Mount Nilgiri
By: Calle Eddy

We are climbing up along the eastern bank of *Kaligandaki River*. There are small pebbles all over our path and towards our right hand side is a black mountain which produces these gravels. In front of us is a naked plateau and behind us *Mt. Nilgiri* looking at us incessantly.

After a short walk, the pebbles disappeared and there appeared very small and round black stones on our way. If we are

---

[84] .Annapurna Area Conservation Project.

to suppose stones that are picked up by people in *Ridi*[85] of *Gulmi* district thinking them as *Shaligrams*,[86] we can no doubt say that here are *Shaligrams* all over the way. On our left is seen a small village with greenery below a landslide-prone hill.

We arrived in a small valley after walking for a long time. It is the valley in the sense that there are hills all around except for the gorge from where *Kaligandaki River* flows ahead. In the middle is a plain area and there are very short thorny shrubs as if they are planted carefully in equal distance. We spent long time enjoying the view at this open and empty land.

Himalayan thorny bushes
By: Lut

We reached '*Tangbe*' village after crossing a small gorge. Our cooks had prepared food at a goat-shed. The tradition here was keeping sheep, hilly goats, goats and mules under the open sky by enclosing the area with a wall all around. Our kitchen is such an enclosure for today. Our crew has collected the goat's excretes at a place to show the kitchen as clean, but the wind is blowing the dust and has troubled us. Near our kitchen, a few *Bhote* brothers have slaughtered two sheep and have chewed half of the raw

---

[85] .An old hilly bazaar of Western Nepal at the bank of Kaligandaki River.
[86] .Ammonite fossils.

meat while chopping. Some of them are making small pieces of meat and some are again filling sheep-blood in the bowels with the help of a funnel. But what everyone is attentive at is chewing the raw meat. Beside them is a big fire, but no one is roasting the meat on it.

After leaving *Tangbe* village, we again saw various kinds of stones such as some pebbles, some like marbles and some sharp gravel. Our shoes were moving over all types of stones.

The seedlings: as if the mountains are growing
By: Lut

Our way was shortened with each of our steps and we reached *'Chusang'* village. The scenery here is really fantastic. The cliffs around us look like old forts. There are fantastic carvings all over the cliffs; some are like remnants of grand palaces and some like the *Janaki temple* of *Janakpur*. Even the cliffs and hills here are full of fantastic craftsmanship of nature.

A view of Chusang: artifact of the Nature
By: Lut

Construction of nature (on the way to Chusang)
By: Patrick Blindman

We had to cross a small steep river after passing through *Chusang* village. I had moved up and down the river with the hope that I can do without putting off shoes, but in vain, and once again I had to tend my stinky socks. After crossing the river we again continued our journey along the bank of *Kaligandaki River*.

They said that *Shaligram* can be found at this place. We have projected our eyes to the shore looking for the *Shaligram*. It is not only the *Nepali*, but also the foreign friends are busy in searching of *Shaligram* with great attention. Whatever stones I had conceived as *Shaligrams* are here all over the way – no need to select but every piece deserves and so we could pick them with a shovel. I am searching for a black and smooth stone with a stripe around as was informed by *Mr. Furba*. Fortunately, I found one. When *Furba* gave it a strike to test, we could see a clear shape of a wheel inside.

"Yes, this is the genuine *Shaligram*" *Furba* said. But the *Shaligram,* which I got very hardly, was broken into two halves and I had to throw away in experiment. The same types of thrown stones are visible around the bank.

Perhaps others too would carry out tests like us.

We continued our searching for *Shaligram* so long as we didn't arrive at a bridge at the foot of the hill leading to '*Chele*'. As we set foot on the bridge to cross the river, we were disassociated with the river-bank and only then we looked at the hills above. Just crossing over the bridge, a steep slope was on the way leading to the village. With the beginning of this slope, the story of *Shaligram* was over.

When we were heading north from *Jomsom,* we were on the western shore of *Kaligandaki River*. When we approached '*Eklebhati*', we came to the eastern shore after crossing a suspension bridge. Now, once again we have arrived on the western shore after crossing a bridge on way to '*Chele*' via '*Chusang*' village.

The scenery near the bridge is wonderful. A part of the river is entered and it passes out under a cliff near the bridge. The scene in which water seems to be flowing through a four sided culvert is really spectacular. How a part of *Kaligandaki River* did carved an artistic door to pass itself through? Similarly, what a terrible dance the river will perform when the whole of the cliff above its door comes down to block it. The river is itself divided into two parts. One of them comes through the shore and the other comes from under the door created by it. The same bridge over the river has two different forms. Half of it is in *truss* style and another half is in the form of *suspension* bridge.

Shaligram: smiling with a wheel
By: Mr. Khagendra Pokharel

We saw seventeen big holes on the cliff far above after climbing a little following the crossing of the bridge. We learnt that before 700 years, people used to live in the holes that looked like big windows of modern houses. In fact, the holes are bigger than the houses of poor people in *Bajhang* district, and are in the same size on a row. *Furba* said there is an inner wall painted with mud. Experts may explain what the truth about it is, but the similar holes in a row on the cliff far above are themselves worth taking a view.

We reached '*Chele*' village within twenty minutes after ascending. They say, in *Tibetan* language, '*Cho*' means '*pond*' and '*Le*' means '*nice*'. Therefore the village was called '*Chele*' as the top of the hill was a better place to see the beautiful lakes of

Kaligandaki. Similarly, according to *Furba*, the meaning of the village '*Chusang*' which we have just left is a '*water pot*'.

Kaligandaki River embracing 'Chele' village in the lap
By: Lut

We have now come on the hotel roof covered with firewood and are looking sometimes towards the *Himalayas* on the south and sometimes towards the cliffs with carvings around us.

Magic of the Nature
By: Calle Eddy

Now, it's only 15.00 in the afternoon. But we won't go further to the uphill. At the place, where our tents are to be hooked, *Japanese* flowers are bloomed that exactly look like butterflies. The wind is blowing stronger, but our tents are safe because of the tall wall. A team of eleven *Americans* has also been mixed with us on the same yard tonight. Although our kitchens, dining rooms and tents are different, we will be sleeping on the same ground today.

Now, we have come to the rooftop of the hotel which is covered by firewood and looking around, from where we can see the magic of the nature on the cliffs which are really carved.

***

PRICE FOR THE HORSE

We had to walk from '*Chele'and we really walked*. After walking the momentous ascend, we left *Kaligandaki River* and followed the '*Ghyakar*' stream. After walking through the graveling path for some time, we began to walk on the path made of carving stone on the cliff to the eastern bank of *Ghyakar* stream. The trail is dusty all over. Our shoes are sunk in the dust when we walk and when we move our steps the dust flies onto our eyebrows. My heart can't distinguish whether we are walking on the eastern bank cliff of *Ghyakar* stream or at *Baletaksar* of *Gulmi* district. While visiting to and form *Tamghas*, we used to call *Baletaksar* as '*Dhuletaksar*'[87] because of the trouble the dust gave us.

The passengers from *Tamghas*[88] come to *Tansen*[89] with dust covering them all over even on their eye brows. Now, we have become like them. Our big group and mules are walking together on this way. Therefore, there is no way to be protected from the dust. All of us have tied a knot behind after covering our mouths and noses with handkerchiefs. Despite all this, the dust has been able to make our sights dimmer. The path is not that sloppy and our steps have been moving forward in a slow motion. The

[87] .'Dhulo' means 'dust' and 'Taksar' means 'mint'; thus the mint of dust = Dhuletaksar in Nepali.
[88] .District headquarters of Gulmi district.
[89] .District headquarters of Palpa district.

Ghyakar village is seen on the lap of the cliff across the river. The big boundary wall built with the labor of the *Ghyakar* residents and the buck-wheat farms enclosed are also seen. The path to *Ghyakar* village including the tunnel like portion carved on the cliff is also visible like a motorable road from here.

We arrived at the upper part of the hill and offered a stone on the *'Deurali'* where a *Buddhist* flag was erected. Form this higher place; we can see the *'Samar'* village faraway. We also saw big and leafy trees in the village. From this faraway place, we thought they are poplar trees. But contrary to our belief, they were *Bhote Pipal*[90] trees, which were grown on the ground of the availability of water. The residents of *Samar* village have grown such big trees along the canal, which has given life to these trees.

Ghyakar village: smiles with buck-wheat flowers.
By: Prateek Dhakal

We can see from the hill that big walls have enclosed all the farms. Earth and stones heaped at a place could build wall in *Mustang*. As there is no rain, nothing happens to walls whether they are that of farm or house. In *Mustang*, it is essential to put walls in the farms either to protect farm from livestock or to protect plants from the gust of the violent wind. There are walls

---

[90] .Populous spices. Poplar trees.

everywhere. A little of greenery is always seen inside the fence—in this kingdom of walls.

In *Nepali* language, '*Samar*' generally means 'war'. But this '*Samar*' was a *Tibetan* word in which '*Sa*' meant '*land*' and '*Mar*' meant '*red*'. If it was in our language, this place was a '*Ratmate*'[91] hillock around *Ridi bazaar* or *Sindhuli*. Now, we are getting ready for a lunch at the *Hotel Annapurna* in '*Samar*' or '*Ratmate*' if we are to call it in *Nepali* language.

A Chorten in Samar village.
By: Lut

Yes, something interesting took place while we entered the hotel for lunch. The entrance to the hotel was not very clean. It had a filthy drain with water flowing. Dung of mule was spared all over as it was a mule track. But when we entered the first floor of the hotel, we found the management of the hotel so standard, beyond our imagination. I was surprised that there was such a grand hotel here. In fact, the inner cleanliness of the hotel was not complainable. Below it are kept horses and mules. There is the '*dain*' undertaken at the yard for threshing wheat. But a floor above is a lodge, hotel or restaurant whatever we call it, which is decorated well in *Tibetan* style.

---

[91] .Red soil.

Now, we have arrived at a place much higher up from *Samar* after completing some short descends and a long ascend. Our path is wide enough like a motorable road and there are shrubs of *Dhupi*[92] above and below the path. We can also see a lot of severed tree-stems. They were said to be felled by the *Khampas*[93] many years after intruding into *Nepal* from *Tibet*. Whatever shrubs we see now are none taller than six feet. All have uniform shapes like *Japanese 'bonsai'*. Now, we are at the top of the hill surrounded by these shrubs with religious banners and flags. A big heap of stones offered by commuters has been gathered at the foot of the flags and banners on the hill-top. We can see a long range of *Himalayan* peaks southwards including *Mount Tilicho*, *Mount Nilgiri* and many other unknown peaks. When we turn to the east, we can see a long range of the *Damodar* peak. Towards the east, there is a naked hill with many layers on whose top stands the *Damodar* peak looking like a crown.

We have arrived at the top with much difficulty. There were the *Himalayan* peaks on the south already, but when *Himalayan* peaks also erupted on the east, the pleasure of our journey was doubled. As I looked towards the west, there was snow on a hill-top too. Although the snowy peak on the west is not permanent, we can see *Himalayan* peaks all around from our way except for the north. I think its fortunate ever to have the opportunity to stand amid *Himalayan* peaks.

The evening is drawing closer. *Patrick* has not been able to walk. Because of his tiredness, his wife *Lut* and *Furba* too are left far behind. *Eddy*, his wife *Rita* and I are ahead of them. We arrived at a village called 'Vena' which had only two houses, but *Patrick* is still behind. Again, we arrived at a village called '*Yamta*' with only one house under a cliff, and *Patrick* is still behind. We are walking slowly waiting for our friends who were left behind. Finally, we came the village '*Syangmochen*' which was pronounced

---

[92] .Junipers Spices, Juniper shrubs.

[93] .Tibetan rebels

easily by all as *'Syangboche'*.[94] We are waiting for our friends by putting our luggage at the *Hotel Syangboche* of the village, *Syangmochen*. But, the presence of our friends is no more visible to the winding path lying too far away. We also hoped that they might have arrived at the turning near *Yamta* village. But, it is almost impossible as they were left too far behind.

Stones offered to the top (Deurali): Tsarang Pass
By: Prateek Dhakal

Perhaps, we should rescue *Patrick*. I sent *Mr. Bhoj Bahadur* to look for a horse. No one was ready to give a horse without giving *NRs.* 500/– even for a short time. *Bhoj Bahadur* informed me this as he returned. I consulted with *Mr. Eddy* and he said "Yes."

Bhoju[95] again went to horseman. *Patrick* and others were found very closer soon after the horse had galloped. He didn't need to ride the horse. But they said that the *Bhote* boy quarreled with them seeking money as the horse was saddled. I was surprised to hear this. These people have been making a living because of the visits of foreigners here. They have been able to see some penny because of their presence here. And today, the same

---

[94] .A popular village near Namche Bazaar.
[95] 'U' sound is added after a person's name to show affection in Nepali culture. Actually he is the same Bhoj Bahadur, one of our kitchen staffs.

people have reached in a state as they have no sympathy over the same foreigner's vulnerable state of health. What a race is man, who only looks for some immediate benefit? The person whom the Great Nepali Poet *Mr. Laxmi Prasad Devkota*[96] had presented as an angel, when the main character '*Madan*' was fallen ill in his great poetic work "*Muna-Madan*," has today inflicted heavily in our hearts. Well, it's a difference in human nature. He gave importance to a few *Rupees*.[97] We sought him giving importance to humanity. The difference is that of hearts and of course, we can't erase the difference between hearts.

Any way, *Patrick* arrived. The arrival of *Patrick* remained more important to us than winning a *Gold Medal* in the *Olympics*. Everybody felt delighted. To mark the happiness, *Furba*, mule driver *Mr. Dilip Bhattachan* and I myself entered into the inn and began to drink local wine with sheep meat. In the evening, we played cards with all our might, but nobody could win except *Temba*. The poor fellow, who ran before us day and night carrying our luggage had won the money enough for buying him a pair of shoes. I was extremely happy to see him winning though I myself lost. Perhaps, Devine hand sometimes does justice.

***

---

[96] .Poet Laureate of Nepalese literature who wrote dozens of books including more than six great epics.

[97] .Currency of Nepal is called 'Rupees'. Generally Rs. 75/- is equal to one US dollar.

On the way to Tsarang

Just as we left *Syangmochen*, we encountered with a small ascend from the very point of departure. After reaching at the top of the hill, we got an easy way for our walk once again. In yesterday's journey we had walked looking at *Himalayan* peaks on both south and east directions. But the range of *Damodar* peak had also stood in a row today with other mountains of the south, contrary to its being seen on the east earlier. This meant that we had come a long way northward. After all, the mountain has not shifted; we are the one who have moved. Walking along, we had moved a lot. The path is felt difficult only until we move. When we begin to walk, the distance of the journey starts decreasing at least by one step, or more. That's why; there is a dictum— "Those who walk reach to the peaks." Everybody is scared in the beginning when one sees a long ascending uphill. Even if we walked uphill counting our steps up to hundred, we will be very high from the foot of the hill.

Syangmochen Pass: another step to higher elevation
By: Calle Eddy

We have been seeing a big village '*Gheling*' towards right hand side of our path. Although we don't have a program to visit this village; it was a place of night-halt for trekkers. *Gheling*, please don't feel angry as we won't visit you this time! We would come someday to see the *Gumba* on your hill-top. Please do not feel sad this time, okay?

We are passing through a rocky surface like a big river-bank without a river. The boulders and the hill-goats grazing are equal in numbers. Very big herds of such hilly goat[98] are moving around in search of grass among the rocks. But there is nothing for them to eat except for a kind of thorny shrubs on this rocky surface. What would they feed on, these innocent creatures. Furthermore, the young uncastreted he-goats are showing their smartness bleating '*Boo-o-o-o*' and chasing she-goats in two feet. From what would they get such sexual energy?

We reached at a small village on the way. I had heard that the name of the village is '*Tamagaun*,' but I was mistaken. Indeed, the name was '*Tamagang*.' In fact, I was thinking that at a place where everything is influenced by *Tibetan* culture in the name of the

---

[98] .'Chyangra' in Nepali.

villages, people and things; how this village can be '*Tamagaun*'[99]? Finally, my suspicion was proved right. The '*Tamagaun*' was the deviated form of '*Tamagang*'. Although it was called *Tamagaun* even by the locals, we could see signboards which mentioned the name as "*Tamagang*" in *Nepali, English* and *Tibetan*.

Now, this is the '*Chhunkar*' village. We found this village with greenery because of *Bhote Pipal* trees grown in the style of a nursery; but having only three houses. It is clearly seen that a big *Chorten* built at the far side of the village has enhanced the beauty of the village. The *Chorten* is painted with soil. But the soil is in five colors. What a pleasant feeling! What a spectacular creation! Flowers of various kinds had blossomed on the same earth. On the same soil had the bitter guard and the sweet papaya or oranges grown. But interestingly, the same earth was divided into soils of five colors here to paint the *Chorten*.

We reached '*Zaite*,' a village with only one house. The only house is everything here, a village, a hotel, a lodge or a restaurant. A terrible dog is looking at us. But it is neither barking nor threatening us nor is it welcoming us by moving its tail. It is lying as if in a serious thought. Perhaps it is also learning to welcome guests by discarding the cow-boy culture. And perhaps it is passing through a transitional phase, exactly like our democracy.

We stood for a long time in front of this house. But we had not halted here to look either at this house or that dog. The *ACAP* has put a signboard beside this house giving information about the paths. This board has traced information in English with names of the paths, distance, time to be taken as well as altitude. Although the map is not as per scale, it has all information needed to us. The *ACAP* has done a useful work in this area. Signboards are installed at every village with their names in *Nepali, English* and *Tibetan*. They indicate the next village and the route to it. It has also established sales centers

---

[99] .Resembling a mid-hill Nepali name which means the 'copper village.'

for selling distilled water. And it has made arrangements for the trekkers to bring back empty cans, cartoons, bottles and cases used by them to *Kagbeni* itself by counting each item. The *Upper Mustang* is very neat and clean with the efforts of *ACAP*. We can only find studs of '*Khukuri Churot*'[100] on the way occasionally. It's clear that the foreigners do not smoke *Khukuri* cigarette. Therefore, without doubt, these studs are the present of the *Nepalese* people. Anyway, we are ourselves responsible for damaging and dirtying anything,— but the *ACAP* was putting a barrier upon our own habits, which made me quite happy.

The path on which we are walking now is like a grand avenue. There are no ups and downs. But the whole area is full of round stones, as in any river-bank in *Terai*.

We arrived in '*Ghami*'. This was a very big village of the high *Himalayan* region. Perhaps, there may be more than 60/70 houses. Here too, we entered into a hotel through a filthy entrance as in *Samar*. Just after ascending to the floor, there was a genuinely marvelous and prosperous hotel. The characteristic feature of this area was hotels nicely decorated in *Tibetan* style on the first floor, and an open space with a water tap fixed for kitchen.

We have sat at a lunch table relaxing ourselves. Our kitchen staffs have been preparing meals at the open space below. The kitchen staffs and our other men have not lagged behind in teasing hotel girls at any places. They are flirting here too, wholeheartedly. But this kind of flirting was something unbearable for us. Perhaps we were accustomed to have gentle flirting and their type of flirting using their hands up to breasts was too much for us. I told *Temba* not to do so. But the fellow would not heed. Rather he would try to convince me— "It's common for us *Bhotes*. Flirting in talks only is not a flirting. Really sir, we need to play with their young breasts."

---

[100] .A brand name of inexpensive Nepali cigarette.

The meals are being prepared and I am looking around in a style of inspection. This area was well developed. In appearance, the houses looking like dull heaps of stone are dirty. But when we go to the first floor, the spacious rooms, decoration in *Tibetan* style and the internal grandeur is very praiseworthy. This is a big thing for this place. They look like tourist-standard restaurant in *Kathmandu*, which is a very good thing indeed.

Soon after departing from *Ghami,* we crossed the *Kaligandaki River* through a suspension bridge. The wind is pushing us from behind and its pressure is also felt to be helping us to climb up the short hill across the river. The place across the river is the same '*Ghami*' and it has been getting a new life. The *Japanese* well-wishers have built the '*Ghami Hospital*' which is a very good hospital.

Various crops have been experimented inside the green-house. Various species of flowers have also been grown. All these creative works have been done under the initiative of a Japanese national, *Dr. Miyazaki* working in the hospital. We heard that *Nepali* doctors have also been deputed. But is it possible that a *Nepali* doctor would come at this place where he can't make money?

We entered into the hospital for a while. There was a beautiful garden built at the premises. We were introduced very heartily with the medical staffs, Japanese doctor *Mr. Miyazaki* and two Nepali nurses *Mrs. Manju Chhetry* and *Ms. Purna Laxmi*, who said they were from *Kathmandu*. We had a conversation for a while regarding cooperation. They sought help in conveying their remembrance to their families and also to take home their letters.

Three midwives meet: Purna, Lut and Manju.

By: Prateek Dhakal

We couldn't stay longer as we had to reach 'Tsarang.'[101] All of us came out of the hospital. The doctor and both the nurses bade us farewell while coming out of the hospital. The beautiful garden before us was left behind at the premises of the hospital and in our share was a tardy uphill climb we had to pass through. The uphill climb is not very steep. We continued our journey and reached at the top of the hill counting each steps.

The path onward is not steep uphill. We are walking along a way which looks like as if open and plain area. The altitude of the mountains has been decreasing and they look like the hills of *Dadeldhura*[102] district as if they are placed by the hands of man. But what is unlike *Dadeldhura* is that there is no greenery around here. There are only thorny shrubs of small plants of uniform size, likes the lumps of excretes of a buffalo. Wherever there is source of water, there are houses and the people have grown *Bhote Pipal* trees. In many places, pleasant sceneries have been formed to satisfy our hearts because of the *Bhote Pipal* trees. We have now understood that *Tamagang, Chhunkar* or *Ghami* whatever we call,

---

[101] .Pronounced as 'Charang.'
[102] .One of the Far Western hilly districts of Nepal.

they are the same series of the interrelationship of water, people and *Bhote Pipal*.

Finally, we arrived at *Tsarang* after passing through a long river-bank like place, but without a river. The situation here is the same. Hotel, *Bhote Pipal* trees and water are interrelated here too.

Japanese flowers at Ghami hospital premises
By: Prateek Dhakal

After putting down our luggage at the hotel of *Miss Maya Bista* who is also the *Chairperson* of *Tsarang VDC*, we went to see the nearby *'Tsarang Dorji Then Gumba'*. They said this *Gumba* is 650 years old, but doesn't look that much prosperous. However, I must be grateful to this day, September 24, the Sunday, which gave me the opportunity to enter into this center of faith.

After entering into the *Gumba*, I knelt down before the immense statue of *Lord Buddha* and lit a lamp in the name of my late mother, *Pavitra Dhakal*. I remembered my mother's face which was seen only in my childhood. Unknowingly few drops of tear came out from my eyes.

Approaching Tsarang village
By: Prateek Dhakal

"I have not performed ritual *'Shraaddha'*[103] in your name, nor so far done any respect that would immortalize your name. Mother, please forgive me. May your soul rest in eternal peace …"

My heart realized my mistakes unexpectedly with repentance. I determined with my heart— "I will light lamps in every *Gumba* in the name of my late mother from now onwards and will perform ritual *'Shraaddha'* as per *Hindu* traditions from this year."

And then I returned to the hotel.

When I returned, our cooks were making preparations for our meals. But the porters had been already engaged in teasing the young hotel girls.

---

[103] .A ritual performed in memory of deceased parents.

Outer view of Tsarang Gumba
By: Lut

Trekkers while resting.
By: Furba

***

THE TRIPLE 'S' OF LOMANTHANG

We are on our journey to *Lomanthang* and we are already gladdened before we left *Tsarang* thinking that we will reach there today. They say it takes only 4/5 hours to reach *Lomanthang* from *Tsarang*. We have nothing to be worried even if it takes 7/8 hours because we will reach there today definitely. Since we do not have further program to go beyond *Lomanthang*, however long it takes to reach there, we won't care. In addition, we will have two more day's rest in *Lomanthang* to heal our tiredness so far. There, we will take a bath happily and will wash the minute clothes unwashed. Then it will give a good rest and the body will be smart. We will have great enjoyment once we reach *Lomanthang*.

We left *Tsarang* with great excitement. We moved ahead by jumping over a turbine which passed water from above to the electricity powerhouse. This turbine is slanted horizontally on the main path like the story of a stick set on the way as a barrier to stop commuters by a *Limbu*[104] boy. We are also moving ahead by jumping over it quickly. The path ahead has no ups and downs and we have to walk on a long stretch resembling river-bank. Yes, because of the area being in the hilly region, a little up and down is no more unnatural. But in this place there is no mentionable

---

[104] .An ethnic community of eastern hills of Nepal. They are famous for their bravery.

113

ascent or the scaring. It is a long plain area like a riverside without a river.

The hills have turned smaller like small spurs. And, all the cliffs have magic of craftsmanship. Every hill looks as if it is carved or sculptured. The hills have forms and images of the feature of nature.

We have already walked half of the way. On the way, we met two healthy horse-riders who went towards *Tsarang*.

"Is the man on the horse the *Mustange Raja*?"[105]— *Eddy* asked me.

Looking to the far horizon....
By: Lut

"Actually, I don't recognize him"— I replied, which discouraged *Eddy*. They wanted to meet the *Mustange Raja*. Therefore, they feared that if the king would not be there as they reach *Lomanthang*.

"No, no, the king is physically an old person. These young men must be some others"— one of our porters, *Temba* interrupted us. They were only happy when I interpreted them in *English* what *Temba* had said. *Eddy* informed me that they had brought one bottle of wine and a souvenir packet with a

---

[105] .The king of Mustang.

photograph of the *Belgian King* and the *Queen* from *Belgium* to offer the *Mustange* king as a matter of gift. Therefore they were worried whether they would be able meet the king and present the gift. They were all happy when it was confirmed that one of the men who just passed was not the king of *Mustang* in terms of his age. I was happy too because *Mustange Raja* is a living history of this period. I had also wished to meet the king when I am here by the chance. I had also lived in *Bajhang*[106] for two years. There is a tradition of addressing as 'Raja' or 'Babu Shaheb' to honor all those with the surname '*Thakuri*.'[107] As the settlement there has more *Thakuris* the social fabric is "Many kings and few subjects". But the case of *Mustang* is different. The *Mustange Raja* is a local king with a history of his own. The only difference we see is that when we hear his name as "*Jigme Parbal Bista*", we remember the *Hindu Bistas* from the mid-hills and the *Terai* with that surname. But in the *Himalayan* region *Bista* and *Gurung* are the branch of the '*Bhotes*' falling under the '*flat nose*' and *Buddhist* communities.

We have to reach *Lomanthang* and we have also the desire to meet the king. There is no option other than to walk if we are to do both the things. Therefore we are walking and now we have been crossing a small stream coming from north-west. We have also been meeting a lot of returning tourists on the way. Foreigners talk to foreigners in such occasional encounters. At such moment, my attention goes towards the person who has come as a *Liaison Officer* from any government office. We introduce with each other, have a little chat then proceed on our journey. After all, trekking is all like this.

The stream we have been crossing now has a small cliff towards its right side and we can see man-made holes on it like one, which they said where man used to live 700 years ago. We can see something written in *Tibetan* script in one of the holes. On the big boulders at the riverbank, something has been written,

---

[106] .A remote district of Far-western Nepal.

[107] .They consider themselves of the Royal caste.

which we can perceive, *"Vote for Tree"* and *"Vote for Sun"*. But nothing has been written on any boulder what the people have got after voting for *'Tree'* many times. Perhaps, as the achievement of the government has been written in the hearts of the people with the letters of tears, there was no need to write on the boulders about that. Or perhaps, it was not written because the general expenditure in enamel paint may have been curtailed to provide relief to the people. Well, it's better not to write about it by anybody. Better not to write than taking pain by writing.

"There comes *Lomanthang* after crossing over the hill"— *Furba* had pointed with his second finger like *Girijababu*[108] long before. In the same excitement I had moved ahead by leaving the group behind, thinking that I will wait for my friends only after reaching *Lomanthang*. But when we crossed over the hill, there came this stream. Again my excitement was cooled down and I began to wait for my friends. The trekkers who were returning said— "It will take 45 minutes hardly".

Why should we fear from a petty distance of a foot since we have walked miles? If we are to calculate from *Jomsom* onwards, we have already walked for four days before which this 45 minute is nothing and why should we fear to walk ahead. Today, *Patrick* has also been walking better and we are out of fear.

Again our journey got continuity on the rocky path, and we really reached a *Dhunge*[109] *Deurali*[110] from where we could see *Lomanthang*. We sat happily on the hill for a long time after offering one stone each on a *Buddhist Deurali* with prayer-flags. We can see small grey hills, which was *Nepalese* territory and the hills with dark color on the other side, was the territory of

---

[108] .The then Nepalese Prime Minister Mr. Girija Prasad Koirala; 'Babu' is added after his name to show some respect.

[109] .Stony.

[110] .Top of a hill.

China. And there was *Lomanthang* a little down of the hill and it is stretched over low land.

Lomanthang: The ancient wall-city which was visited mostly by the people of *Europe*, *America* and other developed countries; but rarely visited by *Nepalese* people themselves!

Lomanthang: The place which is more popularized in abroad; but a very few Nepali people know about its importance and make an odyssey!!

Lomanthang: The place which has been continually successful in earning fame on its own because of its own language, art, lifestyle, history and topography but completely ignored by the majority of Nepali people!!!

Lomanthang:

In spite of my birth in the soil of *Nepal*, due to my own ignorance, I have come so late to you. Though late, I salute you as a latecomer *Nepali*.

We again began our journey and after a little walk, we set foot on *Lomanthang*. It was a big town. There were standard shops, hotels and lodges everywhere. Spaces were enclosed by walls to provide the safe space to hook tents as the trekkers prefer to stay in tents especially. The budge words here were kitchen, dining, toilet and camping site and they were sufficient for running this entrepreneurship in this area. As we were paying *NRs.* 160/- for a bottle of beer on the way, it was *Rs.* 100 in *Tsarang* and now we were at a place where we could find a *Chinese* beer at *Rs* 50, a drastic reduction in market price. The weather is not that cold here. The sun is shining, but the cold wave has compelled us to wear sweaters.

Firewood at the rooftop, Mountains of Nepal and China
By: Lut

We have stayed at the camping site of *Mr. Pema Bista*. The journey has found relief. Perhaps semi relief, we can say, because we have yet to return. But why should I excite myself by remembering our return journey so early, as we have just arrived at our goal.

After down loading luggage from the mules, *Mr. Dilip Bhattachan* again went to look for works. It was said that works of transporting firewood from the highland is found here for the mules.

Indeed, the mules will be free for two days, tomorrow and the day after tomorrow. His logic was right that at least the mules could earn the expenses for their feeding if jobs for them are found. But the *Chhumbis*[111] were saying— "*Dilip* brings firewood free of cost for his *Mitini*[112] and enjoys there". Whatever *Dilip* does is no matter for me. If I wash my socks, it would rather save me from the stinking socks.

I went to the canal to wash my socks. Oh, what a cold water! As if it would numb my hands. Despite the sunshine, it looks as if this wind has brought with it all the cold. I hanged the washed

---

[111] .Mr. Chhumbi and his friends.
[112] .The wife of own Meet.

socks and handkerchief on a rope by making a knot. If we did not tie a knot, wind would blow away our clothes towards *China*.

In the evening, *Mr. Urgen Sherpa* sent someone to invite me. We had become friends after being introduced on the way. When I reached there, Officers from the Ministry of Home Affairs *Mr. Lila Bahadur KC* and *Hari Bahadur KC* who had come as *Liaison Officers, Mr. Urgen Sherpa* himself and *Assistant Sub-inspector* (ASI) of the local *Police* post were waiting for me. Soon after I reached there, we began to drink local beer.

From the right: Author and Urgen with other liaison officers
By: Furba

As we stayed longer, we were to dine and also to sleep there. I sent back *Bhoju* after offering wine when he had come to call me. It was interesting, after all what's there to be taken with us when we die?

There was no difficulty in dining as we were to stay unexpectedly, but the house owner raised a question that blankets will be insufficient to sleep there. We came to know that the owner of that grand hotel was a *Postman*. After having acquaintance with each other, he was not ready to leave us even if we requested to go.

We slept comfortably on a sofa sized bed. It was really a *"sofa-sized-sleep."* We gave it a codename *Triple 'S'*[113]. And thus, the first *Triple 'S'* of *Lomanthang* was completed at an unplanned place, that too was quite unexpectedly.

***

---

[113] Sofa Sized Sleep.

COLORFUL STATUES MADE OF G

It's only 08:00, though we have already had our breakfast. The appointment with the king is only at 16:00, I was thinking about how to spend the time before the meet.

"You can happily play *call-break* sir", *Temba* and others said.

"Is not it better if we went to see the *Namgyal Gumba*?"— The foreigners asked.

Between these two options, I thought the proposal of the foreigners is better. Cards can be played anytime but *Namgyal Gumba* can be visited only when we are in *Lomanthang*. It's not a joke coming to *Lomanthang* time and again. And we can't say we visit it again, because future is uncertain. It's better to have a *darshan* of the *Gumba*. I made a determination in my heart. But did not utter any word about this.

"Is not it possible for us to visit *Namgyal Gumba*?"— I asked *Furba*. *Furba* is an old guide who has come to *Lomanthang* several times with foreigners.

"I have not gone there so far"— he said.

"Why, is it prohibited to visit?"

"That may be the reason, but I am not sure! No one had requested to go there so far and no one had ever been taken to the place. The *Gumba* is not mentioned in the route permit. Therefore we have not gone there."

I looked on the route permit after taking it from *Eddy*. It

121

had only walking route mentioned. There was very small space in the green card to write the '*route*'. But what I realized at once was that there were only names of places mentioned. After all no names of *Gumbas* on the way in which we had a *darshan* were mentioned either. I determined that there was no need to write more after indicating '*Lomanthang*' for this large area and asked the foreigners — "do you really want to go?"

"Can you take us there?" They asked me.

"Please be prepared, I'll come in ten minutes and then we will leave for the *Gumba.*"

In these ten minutes, *Furba* and I went to the *Police Check Post* to register the names of the tourists.

"What is the program today, sir?" The *Sub-inspector* who was acquainted yesterday only, asked me.

"Nothing is special. Now, we are going to see *the Namgyal Gumba* and we will enjoy in the evening. And, yes, do we have any formalities before leaving for *Namgyal?*"— I asked the policemen who were slaughtering a he-goat.

Crossing the barrier
By: Calle Eddy

They laughed. "If you want to go, you can go. We have

nothing to say when sir yourself is accompanying"— the *Sub-inspector* said.

I immediately realized that it was only a rumor that we can't go there. Nobody took and nobody went there and thus a tradition was established. In fact, it is nothing other than *Lomanthang*. Therefore, there is no need to mention specially the *'Namgyal Gumba'* in the route permit card.

We came back within ten minutes and left for the *Namgyal Gumba*. In fact, it is not too far away, it can be seen from *Lomanthang* itself on a nearby hill. We can reach the *Gumba*, when we climb a little uphill after crossing a small stream.

We ascended to the hill and reached at the top. On the top of the hill is the *Gumba* before us and we are standing in front of the *Gumba*'s entrance gate. Two large dogs are barking at us from the edge of the *Gumba*. We are not clear whether the dogs are tied or not as they were a little far. But what has been clear is that no one is looking at us even after the dogs have created such a terror for so long. We came to the conclusion that it means there is no one at the *Gumba* at present. Thinking that it is not meaningful to go up, we diverted ourselves to a nearby village. People came out after we shouted in the village. But there is a big lingual problem between us. Finally, *Furba* himself convinced them saying something which we did not understand. Later, we knew that the main *Lama* was busy in some religious works in his own house and we have to wait for him for a while.

We began to wait for the *Lama* sitting on the hill. In the meantime, the **Belgians** distributed chocolates to children. They also distributed some small toys and took many pictures too. How beautiful the village would have been if there was not poverty. There were small villages on hills high above. We could see some village from here, but they were not seen from *Lomanthang*.

Our waiting was about to end. A *Lama* arrived where we were sitting, carrying *Torma*[114] on a plate from the village below. We

---

[114] .Ritualistic images made of ghee/ flour having religious importance.

all said '*Tashidele*'[115] to him and followed the lazy footsteps of the *Lama* towards the *Gumba*. The large dogs, which were barking kept silence as they saw the *Lama*. In fact, they were also tied with big chains.

Outer view of the Namgyal Gumba
By: Lut

A local girl child
By: Lut

After a long hard work, the *Lama* opened the big door lock and took us inside the *Gumba*. The *Gumba* was of medium

---

[115] .Good morning!

standard, not too prosperous, not too poor, just like the medium class *Nepali* people.

We all lit the lamps, after entering into the *Gumba*. We prayed whatever we knew. The *Lama* showed his solidarity by beating the drum while we prayed. We did not know whether he had beaten the drum as part of our prayer or to awaken *Lord Buddha* during our prayer. But we guessed that it was his goodwill to us.

After the prayer, the *Lama* showed us a separate room where *Tormas* were kept. *Tormas* or the colorful idols of various shapes and sizes made of yak ghee, which are attractive and have religious importance. We watched the ghee idols, as we were spellbound. Wonderfully, ghee, if it is cold makes idols.

An old woman of Namgyal village
By: Lut

There is no fear that it would melt because there was no hot weather. The colorful artistry on ghee in cold was really spellbinding.

After taking photographs in groups at the premises of the *Gumba,* we climbed down by bidding goodbye to the *Lama.*

Naturally, we arrived at the campsite. The meal was prepared. The kitchen staffs set the tables for meal as soon as we reached there. All of us cleaned our hands splashing them in the same pot. We wiped out hands by towels and took our seats on the chair.

Interior courtyard of Namgyal Gumba
By: Lut

Visitors with the Head Lama of Namgyal Gumba
By: Chanda

***

SOME MOMENTS WITH THE
KING OF MUSTANG

It was already 07:00, when we arrived at the camp site after completing the first *'Triple S' of Lomanthang*. The kitchen staffs had kept a bottle of beer for me since yesterday. They handed it to me just as I entered inside. As I was drinking half of the beer after giving half to *Mr. Roop Lama*; *Mr. Pema Bista* came in search of me.

"Is anything the matter?"— I asked him.

"I have arranged an appointment with the king at 16:00 o'clock today, please remember it."

We were all delighted to hear the message from *Pema*. I immediately told it to my foreign friends. They were also delighted and were engaged in arranging gifts. I learnt a lot of things from *Pema* about the process and form of our appointment. As he told us, the foreigners could meet the king by paying a fee of *NRs.* 100 each.

We *Nepalese* didn't have to pay this fee. But we had to take *'Khada'*[116] to meet the king. Where to buy a *Khada?* Where to pay the money? How to fold the *Khada?* Where to offer and how to offer? The procedural questions like these became the matter of inquiries and *Pema* talked all about them. Besides this, he also

---

[116] .A piece of special cloth offered someone to respect his greatness.

127

taught me to walk ahead leading the foreigners at our turn of the appointment.

Now, it's just 08:00 o'clock and we are totally free after having breakfast. The time to meet the king is only at 16:00. Therefore, we headed for *Namgyal Gumba* in order to utilize our leisure time. Now a *Liaison Officer* of another group, a *Nayab Subba*[117] at the *Ministry of Home Affairs, Mr. Chand* has joined our team to *Namgyal*. He said his group is not doing appropriate coordination with him. Therefore, he has been with us participating both in gambling and walking since yesterday.

We returned from *Namgyal* and had our meal, but it's not yet 4:00 pm. Our business is only at 4: pm, the appointment with the king. As again we had a free time, even for a short while, we had no option other than playing cards. One thing is certain while playing cards, *Temba* is always winning.

It's now, 3:30 pm. The **Belgian** friends became ready and came. I also rose from the game. Now *Furba* did not accompany us. We six persons including four **Belgians**, our cook *Mr. Roop Lama* and me left for the palace. But surprisingly, we are moving here and there inside the same house where I had slept a '*sofa sized sleep*' yesterday.

Pema is guiding us. Finally *Pema* took us to the same employee, in whose house I had slept on his request. This sleep was codenamed as *Triple 'S'*. After all the *Postman* was himself the man who sold *Khadas* and tickets for the audience of the king. We bought *Khadas* paying *Rs.* 25/- each. We learnt to fold it and to unfold it before the king. The **Belgians** paid *Rs.* 100/- each there and we came down the stairs. There was a crossroad a little ahead where many shops were available. One of them was *Pema*'s shop. *Pema* and the *Postman* were everything; the king's neighbors, relatives and transactors.

After passing through the crossroads, we are now climbing the stairs of a big but dull house. Perhaps, we reached on the

---

[117] .Head Assistant of Nepal Administrative Service.

second floor. It's quiet inside. Only one person is walking before us besides our group and *Pema*. The unknown person and *Pema* are talking with each other. Perhaps, he might be the official of the palace.

After reaching at a big *mane*, at the turning of the stair, *Pema* left us and showed a door saying,— "Now you can go."

We entered into the room. There on the sofa sized bed at the south-eastern corner of the room, which is decorated in *Tibetan* style, an old man was sitting with a vibrant personality. This man must be the king, I guessed within myself. We are here to meet the king and we are told to go inside a certain room. There was no reason to delay for guessing that he himself is the *Mustange Raja* when there is only one old man with a good personality in the room. But it was a matter of the heart, which itself questioned, guessed and replied.

I went straightly in front of the man. I offered the *Khada* on the table as taught by *Pema* and greeted. The king smiled. A kind of brightness was seen in healthy, vibrant and wide *Mongol* face of the old man. I introduced the members of my group one by one. Each of the persons called by name greeted the king offering the '*Khada*'. After the greeting was over, the king gestured us to sit down. The foreigners sat on the sofa beside the king, and I sat on the chair just in front of him. When I was about to say something about our group, the king gestured me to wait for a while. I was also confused for a short time. The foreigners also felt some uneasiness. But, the matter was that the king would only speak and understand *Tibetan*. The king's son *Gyalchung* always had to be an interpreter during the meeting with the foreigners. But the king had stopped us, because the junior king (*Gyalchung*) had gone out for a moment, when we entered. During this interruption we were offered tea, which was both sweet and had good smell.

Gyalchung came to the room and sat on the chair beside his father. Now, we were facing each other and began to talk. I spoke in *English* about the foreigners and their country *Belgium*. The junior king communicated to his father in *Tibetan*. The king responded it in *Tibetan* which was translated by the son for us. It went on for a long time.

On behalf of the **Belgians**, group leader *Mr. Calle Eddy* presented a gift to the king, a packet attached with the photograph of **Belgian King** and **Queen's** and a bottle of wine from Europe. The king accepted it with a smile and told his son to extend many thanks for it. We found the environment comfortable and informal due to the happy face of the king and the simplicity of the junior king. After all, the junior king was also had his education from *Ratna Rajya Laxmi* campus and *Tri-Chandra* campus of *Kathmandu*. He was ever smiling and easy going young man. After the foreigners presented the gifts, I told to *Gyalchung* in a joke "*Raja*, we have nothing to offer but our sentiments." He immediately replied in *Nepali*, — "It's quite enough, sir" and he assured to meet me in *Kathmandu*. I saw enough potentialities in the *Gyalchung* of *Mustang* to become a good friend.

King of Mustang
By: Lut

After spending about forty minutes in chats, I begged permission with the king to take photographs as per the desire of the **Belgian friends**. The king permitted and photos were taken one after another. The flashing lights of the cameras disrupted our talk for a while. I also told someone to take a photograph of myself having between the *king* and the *junior king* in my own camera.

We came down after the meeting was over. *Mr. Pema Bista* was waiting for us at the courtyard downstairs. I heard him saying in replying to the foreigner's question about this building, "It has 108 pinnacles and 108 rooms." But I forgot to confirm it by asking again. And these pinnacles are not as big as in other temples, but are small as a chimney pot. However, it is not a trifle thing to build such a big house in this remoteness.

We came out through the north gate of the palace. There was a very big *Mane* outside the gate, and the gate itself was big, but not so artistic. The whole palace is hidden under '*lungdars*' and holy banners.

Northern entrance of the palace
By: Prateek Dhakal

The evening is yet to fall on us. There is nothing to do now even if we returned to the place where we sleep. Therefore, we just decided to see the town after coming out of the palace. The town was a little dull-looking because of walls everywhere. When the whole of *Mustang* is characterized by wall, what would this poor *Lomanthang* do alone? In fact, *Mustang* was this *Lomanthang* itself. And, later the district was named from the name of this place.

This day is also to be memorable from now onwards when we got acquainted with the relevance of *Mustang*. I think that this place *Mustang* will be never forgotten because of the walls surrounded everywhere.

I respect you, the '*wall-city*' *Mustang!!!*

The author with the King
By: Calle Eddy

***

ON THE WAY TO MARANG

We were ready to return after staying in *Lomanthang* for two days. While thinking about what to take as a token of *Mustang,* we found *Shaligram,* some *Chinese* biscuits and chocolates, mattress of wool and cloth as best. I had already bought yesterday some *Chinese* chocolates and biscuits described as *army's snacks* from the front side of the palace after the meeting with the *king.* But the woolen cloth was yet to be bought. I went out in search of it and found it at a shop. But I was astonished to see the owner. The same man who was selling *Tibetan* ornaments carrying a small bag at our campsite the day when we reached *Lomanthang* and who had vexed *Eddy* time and again by begging for photographing him with the *Polaroid* camera with words, *"One more please"* was the owner of that big shop. The woman who begged with us medicines was his wife. After all, the same person was the shopkeeper who I had myself scolded as he had troubled the tourists by asking for photographing him.

We began to return as my shopping was completed after buying the woolen mattress from the shop of the same naughty owner. The mules were to go to *Tsarang* through the path we had returned last time. But we were to go finally through another way, which would take us to the *Samduling Gumba* and *Marang.* The **Belgian friends**, *Chhumbi* and *I*, a total of six persons stared our journey as *Furba* was to delay for a while to finish payments including that of men, luggage and other things. *Furba* bade us good-bye and suggested, "Please move ahead, I will arrive very soon." We took to the southwest direction though a riverbank like path.

We are passing through a naked highland moor. On a faraway hill, a big herd of sheep is moving covering the whole of the hill. A drinking water pipe was laid along the path we had to travel. We can see water leaked in many places on the way. The potholes made by the leaking water on the sand look like water-wells in *Terai* region of *Nepal*. After walking for a while, we have reached a place from where we can't see *Lomanthang*. But are we following the correct route?

"I have come for the first time; I don't know the way" said *Chhumbi*. What could we do except being confused, when the person who led us was in confusion. Then we neither took rest nor ceased to look back frequently with the hope that if *Furba* is coming. We are heading towards southwest through a very long stretch of riverbank like land. To our south and west are a small hill and a naked hill respectively. We are about to arrive at the foot of the naked hill of the west. The snow has covered the top of the hill. Did we really loss our way? We came to the conclusion that there is no meaning to cross the snow on the western hill. Perhaps, we must cross the short hill towards the south. All of us sat on the stone and engaged ourselves in serious discussion.

We are discussing about the way though we are all ignorant of it. It is also evoking laughter in a way, as we are searching our way on the basis of logic. Is it possible that logic can show our way? I said, "Let's go to the foot of the western hill, perhaps we can find a way leading to downhill which we may not notice from here." But *Patrick* did not agree. He said, "Didn't you see? The path has ended and we have to cross the southern hill."

We saw a human shape on the far away hill while we were ready to leave to the south agreeing with *Patrick's* insistence. We all began to walk towards the direction.

"That is not a man, but a stone,"

"That is not moving"

"Don't you see? It's a man, it's walking."

These were some logics for and against of it. We waited for the image for a long time sitting on the river–bank like place. There is nothing on the land here except for a kind of grasshopper, which makes a sound 'Pota-t-tota,' and flies by showing it's colorful wings.

The image was in fact a man, which was now seen clearly. Finally, we came to know that it was *Furba* himself and soon he arrived near us. We were quite assured now, with the hope that *Furba* may take us wherever we have to go. But when he arrived, he said— "I don't know the way, because I have not passed through this way."

Furba's arrival could not end our confusion. At the end, we were obliged to pass though the low hill of the south as told by *Patrick* and began to climb the hill after crossing a small rivulet at the end of the sandbank.

After reaching at the top of the hill we could see an infinite range of low hills on the south. We ourselves understood that there is no difficult ascent or descent today and our walk will not be difficult. When we saw impressions of footsteps of both horses and men, *Patrick* happily said, "Finally, we are on a correct path. The eleven *Americans* we met yesterday must have returned this way. These are their foot–steps. If we were to follow what you said we would have been lost!"

We crossed tens of hillocks passing through some high and some low land, alternately. We saw a herd of sheep before us. As we were looking around with an intention of finding our way by asking to a shepherd, we saw two men on a far away hill. When we called them with a loud voice, they ran still far away, we could not ask them anything.

Again, we are passing through slope with thorny shrubs. Down at the foot of the hill, an old man is driving five horses.

Perhaps, he wants to take the horses somewhere after grouping them. But the horses are defiant and are troubling the old man by running towards five different directions. As he was the only man we had found luckily after a long time, we had thought that we will ourselves call him when we reach just above him. But when he saw us he himself asked us— "Where would you go?"

"We are to go to *Samduling Gumba,* is this the way?" *Furba* replied his question as his own question. Then, *Furba* and the old man talked for a long time with loud voices— one from the hill and the other at the foot of the hill.

Later, *Furba* told us "We have completely lost our way. There was a different way to go to the desired *Gumba.*"

In fact, whichever way I had told them to look for after reaching a foot of the hill, was the correct way. The old man had said, "Nothing is wrong as yet. You move ahead, straight ahead, and you can reach a village after a long time. You can also find a way to *Gumba* from the village."

"Who was correct?" I teased *Patrick.* He just laughed. In fact, we have lost our way because of *Patrick's* insistence. Though I could not insist as it was something I didn't know, my logic was proved correct.

We are passing through terraced layers of the hills. There are hills, which contain sands. We are walking in a hilly area, but with a feeling of sinking shoes in sand as it is in the riverbanks of *Terai* region. After a continuous walk, we arrived at the peak of a small hill and there we begin to eat tearing our lunch packets. A big descent towards the downhill is seen behind us and we have to go down to arrive at a big sandy bank. This slope downhill is strewn with rocks and we are sitting with our backs towards it to protect ourselves from the thrust of the strong wind blowing from that direction. But the wind would not let us eat. It brings dust and sand to mix into our lunch. After all, we could not resist. Then we climbed down a little backward from where we came as we were not allowed by the wind to eat any more and sat with the support of one thorny shrub each and emptied our lunch packets.

Although our way is downhill descent but it has no steep slope. Therefore I came down without stopping with the support of a stick. But the foreigners are moving ahead with much fear. There is a fear of hitting others with stones that roll while walking. A stone rolling from above would hit other stones pushes them downward with it. This scene is both interesting and dangerous. We came down with much cautiousness.

Now, we have to walk along a sandy bank. A real sandy bank but no river is seen around. In fact, such river-less sandy banks are also a special feature of *Mustang*. After walking for a long time, we arrived at a place where we found the herders grazing their cows. They begged for money to drink wine. None of us gave them money and moved ahead along a canal to the top of the buckwheat field.

Now, we have been moving forward through a buckwheat farm irrigated by a canal. We see a beautiful village in front of us. The beauty of the scenery has further enhanced by the bumper crop of buckwheat. Very beautiful houses are seen. We also began to see people busy in works. And, we really approached in the village. The name of the village, we arrived after crossing innumerable hills from *Lomanthang* was– *Marang*.

The sheeps of the Himalayas: transporting food grains and salt
By: Calle Eddy

We asked the residents of *Marang* about the *Samduling Gumba*. They pointed toward it with fingers. The *Gumba* was at a foot of the cliff, a little westward.

"Do you want to go there?" I asked *Patrick*. He was too tired already. Therefore, he did not show interest to walk backward. All other said —"It's enough."

If we have come along the right path, we would have reached this village after visiting the *Gumba* first. But as we first arrived at this village, we had to walk to the opposite direction to the *Gumba* and to return to this village on the way to *Tsarang* for night halt.

We were not to go to the *Gumba* Because of tiredness. We took our way by bidding good-bye to the *Gumba* from this far. This *Marang* village was bigger than what we had seen it to the beginning. This village was heading towards gradual prosperity because of farms, some greenery and electricity facilities.

We are now going to a suspension bridge on the way to *Tsarang* after crossing *Marang* village. To our right hand side is a cliff and on the top of it is also the kind of big hole that may be said to be inhabited by human being 'once upon a time.' The hole has also window frame and a small door. The beam over the door is also seen from downward. This must be a place where man in the past had really lived. Otherwise, who would have erected such a stone wall and put a wooden window on that cliff?

We also left *Marang*. We moved ahead along the horizontal path after crossing the bridge and reached *Tsarang* for a night-halt walking along the canal that led to the turbine. Earlier, we had seen *Tsarang* from a lower place. Today when we saw it from a higher place *Tsarang* looked more beautiful. *Tsarang* is in fact beautiful and a wish emerged in the heart suddenly for more clarity in its beauty.

Tsarang village from the top
By: Prateek Dhakal

We again went to the very hotel of *Miss Maya Bista*, which we had known earlier. Our friends had not come yet. Where have they gone? Perhaps, they began to flirt somewhere and have not realized that it is being late.

***

CLIMBING UP A CLIFF
ON FOUR FEET

In fact, we had a different way to return. We wanted to go to *Muktinath* via *Dhi, Yara, Tange* and *Tetang* from *Lomanthang*. But as we heard that the way of that route is too difficult as we have to cross a river and have to walk 10/12 hours with pack lunch to reach a place for night-halt, the **Belgian friends** said— "Well, let's return from the same way through which we came here." As for me, I wanted to walk along new routes, however difficult they may be, because of my desire to see new places. But my choice had no place after the relevant people lost their courage. The **Belgians** were also adequately influenced as most of the groups were seen returning from the same route as they had heard that some days ago, a group heading for *Dhi* met with an accident. We arrived at *Tsarang* via *Marang* by changing our usual route for one day as part of our return through the usual route.

After leaving *Tsarang*, we arrived at *Ghami hospital* through the same way and looking the same old things on the way. The *Patrick Blindman couple* presented many sets of needles and thread needed to sew human skin as well as some equipment for surgery to the hospital. The *Call Eddy couple* presented many pairs of eyeglasses. The exchange of assistance as well as heartiness and gratitude were expressed without sitting. Our team moved ahead with a mission of having lunch at *Ghami* village. But I stopped there for a while, as I was to take letters written by the two nurses to their homes.

Conversation with Dr. Miyazaki
By: Lut

It took long to get the letters and I had to wait for a while. I was attracted by the garden in the hospital compound watching at the bloomed sunflowers and *Japanese flowers* grown there. In between I had talks with *Dr. Miyazaki*, but all incomplete. He could not speak English well and I was also unable to speak *Japanese* well. Both of us were imperfect. Talking with much difficulty with him, I waited the nurses to complete their letters.

I was coming alone out of the hospital carrying letters written by two nurses to the two families. I headed for *Ghami* village after crossing the *Kaligandaki Bridge.* But I had headed for the eastern river bank losing a little of my way. After passing through a tunnel like place made of wall, I encountered a terrible dog. Thank God, it could not harm me, but I almost lost my senses because of fear from it. I am in the middle of the village, but nobody is seen around. There are not many houses either. Moreover, I don't know in which house the meal is being cooked for us. These high walls block the way, and I am obliged to follow this tunnel-like alley made by walls on both sides. Finally, I arrived at the right place after making a round to the east and north parts of the village.

I found all our people including the kitchen staffs. But I did not tell anyone that I was lost. Why should I evoke them laughter? Rather I thank the terrible dog, which didn't even bark at me with its unlimited mercy towards me.

After having lunch, we left *Ghami* too. The path and sceneries ahead are all the same, and the only difference is that the villages that came last while coming from *Jomsom* are now coming first. Things on the right then are now on the left.

We are moving ahead across the one house village of *Zaite*, the village with three houses *Chhunkar* and *Tamagang* heard as '*Tamagaun.*' To our left below is seen the *Gheling* village in a considerably big size. We don't have night-halt at this village either coming or going.

Gheling, we have a strong bond of love for you whether we stay or not; whether we touch you or not.

We arrived at *Syangmochen* at about 4:00 pm. We decided to spend the night here. As all of us were willing to stay in rooms, there were no hassles of hooking our tents. The kitchen staffs went towards the kitchen. Others headed for the inns, and it began just with the onset of evening.

I had got a headache in the morning because of yesterday's exhaustion. But we didn't have time for rest. Therefore I left *Syangmochen* early in the morning with my group, carrying a piece of aching head over a quite well body. We arrived at *Samar* village for a lunch after crossing one village of *Yamta*, and two-household village of '*Vena.*'

Trekkers with the teachers of Samar school
By: Eddy

Finally, we had to leave *Samar* and so did we. When we arrived at a hill-up, we met other 2/3 big groups who were coming uphill. The hilltop at that time was like a bus stop for us. We also chatted about the same thing and then we laughed. The goal was different; they headed towards the north and we to the south.

The *Ghyakar* village across the *Ghyakar River* was seen again to our right hand side. Again the dusty path resembling *Baletaksar* came under our feet. As we moved ahead, there came the *Chele* village where we had a night-halt last time. But it is not time yet for night-halt.

Now the *Chusang* village came. There is still much time of the day. Therefore, we headed for *Tetang* village to stay in a new place. We are heading east following a canal. We had been working towards *Tetang* watching the sceneries of beautiful apple orchards, big but pruned *Bhote Pipal* trees grown from the moisture of the canal and the miraculous craftsmanship on the cliffs.

Mirage!! A tree in between desert
By: Prateek Dhakal

We arrived at *Tetang* village in the evening when it was quite dark. We were to stay for the night in a house below a big cliff. Tents were hooked for the guests at the yard inside a fence. *Furba* and I were to sleep inside the sitting room of the owner. All other staffs were to sleep in the kitchen room. Our hunger was removed and tiredness gone after eating two dishful of fresh popcorn just taken from the maize field, in the kitchen room. We had our dinner in the evening for dinner's sake.

We again arrived at *Chusang* after leaving from *Tetang*. Yesterday, we had come through the *Chusang* across the river, but today we arrived at *Chusang* after crossing the river directly. We are walking along a path with pebbles constructed above a cliff on the eastern bank of *Kaligandaki River* and our goal for today has been *Tangbe* village.

We saw *Tangbe* village from far away. We can see from here an apple orchard at the *Mt. Nilgiri's* peak on the top. In other words, the *Tangbe* village looked from here as if sitting proudly wearing a cap of *Mt. Nilgiri* with the feet of apple orchard.

We again arrived at the banks of the *Kaligandaki River*, as we moved. We have now two options before us— to reach *Kagbeni* along the banks of *Kaligandaki River* or to reach there through the path made above a cliff. We had to climb uphill for a while if we go through the *Kaligandaki* river-bank, as we did not have to walk uphill and had opportunity to search *Shaligrams* on the river-bank.

Carving in mountain
By: Calle Eddy

Now, we are no more in-group. All are scattered alone to search the *Shaligram* around the riverbank. We had to cross the water in many places. We were now alone because some took out their shoes other didn't; some searched *Shaligrams* near them and others ventured far away which divided our group. As I didn't take out my shoes and walked in water, I came very near to *Kagbeni* sooner than the friends. When I came near, the riverbank was seen far below and *Kagbeni* far above on the hill which would make us hold our caps even to look at. And now...... OMG! From where to go up?

I was confused. There is no any way around to climb up. Some unclear small trial is seen on the cliff above. Is that the way? Oh, that looks very dangerous. We can't even ask for water when we fall down from there. Is this the way we have to go through?

I looked back at my friends. They were still too far. The situation was that it would have been tiring even if I wanted to wait for them. *Kagbeni* is just above my head, but from where to go there? I saw two horsemen on the riverbanks coming from the south towards me. I waited for them and finally they arrived near me. I asked them the way to climb up. The path had turned into a deserted, dangerous trail without any signs of a path as it was not walked along by trekkers and was only used by the locals occasionally. And now we had to go up hill through the very path.

I began to climb up the hill through the trace. If any steps were not in proper place I will fall straightly down on the river bank. This path was more difficult, dangerous and narrow above than it looked from below. I was worried about the **Belgian friends** more than it looked me as long as I was walking through this path. How would the **Belgian** elderliness who come from a country just 30 meters above from the sea level pass through this path which was frightened us to walk through even if we were born, grown up and had played in the hills?

I completed the way with a great fear and arrived at *Kagbeni*. The place for our night halt was arranged in the same place as earlier. When I arrived, I told the kitchen staffs to go to see towards the path. Two of them went to that direction. I had washed my shoes and lay to dry but could not come out with naked feet as the mule carrying my slippers had not arrived. I was also tired, but my heart was not assured unless they arrived in the hotel. I waited very impatiently.

Near to the Heaven: Challenging trekking & Rarest experience
By: Prateek Dhakal

The ***Belgian friends*** arrived vary late. Their faces were fed up. The wealthily grown up ***Belgian trekkers*** who had never seen such a dangerous ascend were extremely frightened. They had arrived dragging their bodies. Walking at places in four legs! In some places, our staffs had also escorted and carried them over their shoulders. I thought that I had made a good decision to send them back to bring them. As I learnt, *Patrick* was more afraid than others. But *Eddy* and *Rita* were smiling, as it was their habit. A smile of victory after a difficult journey! A smile of achievement that has forgotten the efforts!

"All of us have arrived at *Kagbeni* without any harm whatever trouble we faced or however fear we felt. After all what is at hands is the reality of the present. Look *Patrick,* it's the same thing whether to almost die or not to die. Therefore, stop worrying and try to make the dangerous experience of trekking as your own and earned property"— I convinced *Patrick* as an intimate friend and he looked as if he was convinced.

Finally we conquered: Calle Eddy and Patrick
By: Prateek Dhakal

The foreigners were to sleep in the rooms even today, and

the kitchen staffs in the kitchen itself. At the end, there was no room for *Furba* and me. A tent was hooked for us on the plain ground enclosed by wall behind the house. Only two of us were to sleep like '*tourists*' in a tent today. After all, we '*black*' tourists had no option other then to sleep in the tent, when '*white*' tourists themselves preferred to sleep inside the house.

***

A DAY IN MUKTI-KSHETRA

It's not that we can't come to *Muktinath* straightly from *Tetang*. But we have already come to *Kagbeni* yesterday in order to ease our way by avoiding a possible ascend, as we had to cross a 4000 meters high pass while coming that way. We were almost stranded while climbing uphill to *Kagbeni* from the *Kaligandaki* riverbank when we tried to avoid the *pass* to *Muktinath* from *Tetang*. Fortunately, we arrived at *Kagbeni* yesterday and today we are leaving for *Muktinath* shrine after having breakfast.

We saw a signboard at the middle of the market with the message '*Way to Muktinath*' inscribed on a wooden board, and installed by the *Ministry of Tourism*. At least, the government has shown its presence here. I was happy even to see an old wooden board losing its color. It was because I am a government employee. This *Ministry of Tourism* always used to stay idle by only helping the *NAC*[118] misusing funds. Or it used to stay sorting out names of *Liaison Officers* to be sent for mountaineering expeditions in some leisure. How did it get this leisure to install a board? With a surprise, I moved ahead. I didn't tell anyone about my sentiments. Why should I make the mockery of own self by disclosing it?

We crossed the windmill of the *NEA*[119] and now we are moving our steps to uphill on its gentle slope. Before us, a boy is

---

[118] .Nepal Airlines Corporation.
[119] .Nepal Electricity Authority.

driving cows of the size of goats in *Terai*, perhaps to graze them. What is there to graze? There are stones everywhere and he is hitting the cattle by picking up these stones. A cow herder he is, so he is singing song without stopping, but all of them are the *Hindi*[120] songs. He does not know any of the songs more than a few lines. But he is swinging on his own voice looking many times towards us with the hope that we be amazed in his art. We are neither amazed nor have not stopped walking.

After a long time, the boy removed his goat-sized cows from the way and we had chance to go ahead of them. Otherwise, his cows and horses were continually blocking our way.

We could enter the *Muktinath* valley, when we cross three upward climbs, the first one exactly similar to what we see before us when we look towards the way to *Muktinath* from the *Kagbeni* bazaar. We also arrived at a place called *Khinga* (*Khingar*) in two hours walk from *Kagbeni*. We could found out that this place was *Ward No. 7* of the *Muktinath VDC* as per the signboards of hotels and restaurants. But the boards have also created confusion to the outsiders like us. Some boards have '*Khinga*' and some others have '*Khingar*' as the particular name of this place. Which one is correct? Although, this is a question, but we didn't waste our time to find it out and we moved ahead thinking that both are correct.

We saw commercial houses right from *Khinga*. Hotels, restaurants and shops selling shawls, caps and other hand-woven clothes were on the way. We reached '*Jharkot*' in a short time. *Jharkot* was still bigger commercial center. But all the business is related to tourism. There were very big hotels with signboards that read availability of hot and cold shower twenty four hours a day as well. Other shops were also neatly decorated. We could reach the *Muktinath* shrine through a path leading via villages and settlements once we reach *Jharkot*. The whole *Mukti-Kshetra*[121]

---

[120] .Indian.

[121] .'*Kshetra*' is pronounced as '*Chhetra*' which means area or land. *Mukti-Kshetra* means the holy land of salvation.

is seen as an enchanting valley. Very high and naked hills on the north, a snow clad mountain just above the *Muktinath* temple and the whole *Himalayan* range on the south. The only open area is to the west from where we are coming. But this place is enclosed even on the west by the mountains across the *Kaligandaki River*. Therefore, the *Muktinath* shrine was seen from the entry point as an enchanting valley. Moreover, a low hill was erupted on the deep valley looking like an earthen idol on a dish. Looking at the small hill in the middle, we feel as if it is a sapling of a mountain, which has been just planted and will grow up to, become a big mountain.

We reached at the *Muktinath* bazaar very near to the *Muktinath* temple. Hotels, lodges, shops everywhere and as for people there were '*whites*' more than the local people. There are shops of *Tibetan* ornaments and curio spread along the way. There are business activities everywhere. All the businessmen are busy. Tourism industry had really thrived in *Mustang*. As the area up to *Muktinath* from *Kagbeni* was considered the lower *Mustang*, it was crowded with *Europeans* and *American* people. The prohibited area begins above than this and one *Liaison Officer*[122] was to be deputed by the government among its mid-level employees for the trekking teams. As *Muktinath* area was open to all, tourists would throng this place in great numbers.

We had arrived here at about eleven o'clock in the morning. But we could not find a place to sleep, as all the hotels were full.

We found a five-bedded common room at a hotel with much difficulty and booked it for the foreigners. These hotels and lodges would also give priority to guests who would have their meals at their own hotels as far as possible. Those living in tents and those only sleeping here after eating their own meals were regarded as *second grade* here. We have a sole team of kitchen staffs; therefore we are facing a *second grade* treatment here today.

---

[122] .Now this system is cancelled and foreigners can visit *Upper Mustang* without taking a *Liaison Officer*.

Our kitchen is too far away. The staffs bring *nanglo*[123] set with prepared meals and snacks from there. They also sleep in the room that is called kitchen. In the end, *Furba* and *I* are the only ones not to get space to sleep, always. Even today, two of us have no fixed place for sleeping.

We had no additional problem for the time being when we found the kitchen and a room with five beds. We have kitchen to cook and space for guests to sleep, the rest remains for later. After all, the night has not fallen on us yet.

We headed for the temple area after lunch. Attempts were made nicely to decorate the stone-steps. We entered into the temple premises moving the big *mane* at the gate of the temple. Efforts were made to grow plants by letting a board of these who plant them to encourage tree plantation. Now, we have entered into a garden amid a desert land. Everywhere, there are life giving greenery, trees and plants. It's not good to compare this greenery of gardens elsewhere. Piercing the heart of the desert whatever had been done here is highly valuable. Every efforts made here are really praise worthy.

We reached at the premises of the temple. This is mid-day, but the temple is not a quite place. We are about fifty people even now including devotees and *Brahmins* [124] reciting religious texts. Offerings are made in the sacrificial fire and recitals from religious texts are continuing. But the meaning of recital is different for each. Some recite for religious devotion and some for earning a few *Rupees.*[125] However, this area is echoing with the sacred recitals.

I went towards the 108 taps to circumambulate them from the right. The **Belgian friends** were rejoicing by taking

---

[123] .Big and round winnowing device made of bamboo.
[124] .The highest class of people according to *Hindu* class division. They are supposed to work as priests.
[125] .Nepali currency.

photographs. I did not think it better to take a bath because the water was cold and the space was open and began to sprinkle water on my head from each of the taps. At the same time a group of bald head *Buddhist* monks came and began to sprinkle water on their heads likewise. Together we went round the temple and entered in the place by opening a curtain where there was the deity. A *Buddhist Jhuma*[126] helped us to perform our worship as a priest. The foreigners had to see it from outside. But there is no stern restriction as in the *Pashupatinath* temple in *Kathmandu*.

I came out after completing the *darshan*. I was thinking myself fortunate today to find myself in the sacred and common shrine of *Hindus* and the *Buddhists*. People from both religious sectors come and express the devotion of similar nature. They perform the worship in similar ways. The temple is regarded as the *Hindu* temple, but the priest used to be a *Buddhist Jhuma*. What a great correlations! What a great interdependency! The *Lord Muktinath* was really the liberator especially for all of us. My heart bowed myself before the supreme reign of the *Almighty* without any further logic.

After coming out of the temple, we moved towards the area where *stupas* were to be built with devotion. All of us built *stupas* like that built by children putting stones one after another and we moved to the temple of *Jwalamai*.[127]

The *Jwalamai temple* can be called both '*Temple*' and '*Gumba*,' which has also *Buddhist Jhuma* as priest. The *Jwalamai* deity is just below the huge statue of *Lord Buddha* inside a house decorated in *Gumba* style. I had thought that the *Jwala*[128] might be bigger. But the reality was different. When we see it after pulling the curtain on the wired net we can hear and see the bubbling water and an unabatedly burning flame of fire side by side. This was regarded as the *Goddess Jwalamai*. The strange thing is a flame of fire burning

---

[126] .A nun.

[127] .'*Jwala*' means '*flame*' and '*Mai*' means the '*mother*'.

[128] .Flame.

continued without any mundane support. Thank *God*, we bow respectfully towards your miracles.

The holy fountains of Muktinath
By: Calle Eddy

We again arrived at the main gate of the temple moving all the *manes* that were hanged on the way as we returned. We had completed the circumambulation of the *Mukti-Kshetra* and the only thing we had to do now was to return to the hotel. But the problem is still intact, what to do after returning to the hotel? There is no place for me to sleep.

The hoteliers here were not so desirous to provide lodging or feeding to us as far as they get foreign trekkers. In a way, these people here are as arrogant as the hotels[129] in *Mugling*[130].

"Where do you sleep?"— *Calle Eddy* asked as soon as I arrived at the hotel.

"Not yet fixed"— I said.

He said— "There are five beds in our room. We sleep in four beds. One will be vacant. You can sleep on it, won't you? You should not feel uneasy."

The other three persons also had seen me feeling uneasy.

---

[129] .Small hotels providing Nepali *Daal-bhat*.
[130] .A small town on the way to *Pokhara* from Kathmandu.

A frank woman *Lut (Mrs. Patrick)* moved forward and said openly— "We sleep on our beds in sleeping bags. We will have no '*special*' program when we are two couples in a single room. You can sleep on the vacant bed without hesitation. But, please sleep in the sleeping bag turning to other side. And if you can, please help us by falling asleep very soon, isn't it good?"

All of us broke into laughter. *Lut* also laughed. Now, the problem was resolved. We all five people were to sleep in a common room. The remaining *Furba* got some space for him in the kitchen. After it was settled, one of the staffs brought my bag in the room occupied for the guests.

After the place for sleeping was fixed, I felt free and went to the bazaar for a stroll. There is nothing to worry now!

Farewell to the trekking crew
By: Lut

We will leave for *Jomsom* tomorrow morning. It will take maximum four hours to reach *Jomsom* after reaching *Eklebhati*. It will not take more than that because the path is descending to the down hill. And we will fly in a plane to *Pokhara* after a night's enjoyment in *Jomsom*. Then, towards *Kathmandu* on the *Phulpati day,*[131] there will be everything including my children. A

---

[131] .Seventh day of the greatest Hindu festival *Dashain*.

joyful *Dashain* when I will have the opportunity to talk to others about my visit to *Mustang*. What more things I need to be done? After all, I have already bought the famous apples and brandy of *Khurpani*[132] from *Mustang*!

---

[132] .Apricot